C O N N E C T I N G

TEACHERS
STUDENTS AND
STANDARDS

Strategies for Success in Diverse and Inclusive Classrooms

ASCD MEMBER BOOK

Many ASCD members received this book as a
member benefit upon its initial release.

Learn more at: **www.ascd.org/memberbooks**

ASCD cares about Planet Earth. We are printing this book through
The Sustainable Forestry Initiative® program, which promotes
responsible environmental behavior and sound forest management.

CONNECTING

TEACHERS
STUDENTS AND
STANDARDS

Strategies for Success in Diverse and Inclusive Classrooms

Deborah L. **Voltz**

Michele Jean **Sims**

Betty **Nelson**

 Alexandria, Virginia USA

1703 N. Beauregard St. • Alexandria, VA 22311-1714 USA
Phone: 800-933-2723 or 703-578-9600 • Fax: 703-575-5400
Web site: www.ascd.org • E-mail: member@ascd.org
Author guidelines: www.ascd.org/write

Gene R. Carter, *Executive Director;* Nancy Modrak, *Publisher;* Scott Willis, *Director, Book Acquisitions & Development;* Julie Houtz, *Director, Book Editing & Production;* Leah Lakins, *Editor;* Greer Wymond, *Senior Graphic Designer;* Mike Kalyan, *Production Manager;* Circle Graphics, *Typesetter*

All Web links in this book are correct as of the publication date below but may have become inactive or otherwise modified since that time. If you notice a deactivated or changed link, please e-mail books@ascd.org with the words "Link Update" in the subject line. In your message, please specify the Web link, the book title, and the page number on which the link appears.

ASCD Member Book, No. FY10-8 (July 2010, PSI+). ASCD Member Books mail to Premium (P), Select (S), and Institutional Plus (I+) members on this schedule: Jan., PSI+; Feb., P; Apr., PSI+; May, P; July, PSI+; Aug., P; Sept., PSI+; Nov., PSI+; Dec., P. Select membership was formerly known as Comprehensive membership.

PAPERBACK ISBN: 978-1-4166-1024-3   ASCD product # 109011

Also available as an e-book (see Books in Print for the ISBNs).

Quantity discounts for the paperback edition only: 10–49 copies, 10%; 50+ copies, 15%; for 1,000 or more copies, call 800-933-2723, ext. 5634, or 703-575-5634. For desk copies: member@ascd.org.

Library of Congress Cataloging-in-Publication Data

Voltz, Deborah L., 1961-
  Connecting teachers, students, and standards : strategies for success in diverse and inclusive classrooms / Deborah L. Voltz, Michele Jean Sims, and Betty Nelson.
    p. cm.
  Includes bibliographical references and index.
  ISBN 978-1-4166-1024-3 (pbk. : alk. paper) 1. Inclusive education—United States. 2. Classroom management—United States. 3. Multicultural education—United States. 4. Teaching—United States. 5. Special education—United States. 6. Children with disabilities—Education—United States. I. Sims, Michele Jean, 1952- II. Nelson, Betty Palmer. III. Title.
  LC1201.V65 2010
  379.1'54—dc22
                                        2010010846

20 19 18 17 16 15 14 13 12 11 10   1 2 3 4 5 6 7 8 9 10 11 12

CONNECTING

TEACHERS
STUDENTS AND
STANDARDS

Strategies for Success in Diverse and Inclusive Classrooms

PREFACE

Dorothy Noble is a 6th grade language arts teacher. She has a diverse mix of students in her class, which includes English language learners, students who are gifted and talented, and students who have disabilities. Ms. Noble always has taken pride in being a good teacher. Lately, she has felt over-whelmed by competing demands to help all of her students meet the same academic standards and demands and to accommodate the needs of an increasingly diverse population of students.

Derrick is a student with learning disabilities in Ms. Noble's class. His literacy skills are at a beginning 4th grade level. Vickie, another student in the class, functions more like a beginning 9th grader. In addition to the obvious skill differences between these students, there is great diversity with respect to how these students learn best. Vickie and Derrick represent just the tip of the iceberg in terms of the range of students in Ms. Noble's class. During the spring, all of Ms. Noble's students will be expected to take the same state assessment designed to measure student performance against established standards for 6th graders. Ms. Noble is left wondering, "What is the best way to accommodate each student's individual learning needs while simultane-ously teaching the same standards for everyone?"

Ms. Noble is not alone in her quandary. With the passage of the No Child Left Behind Act, there has been increasing emphasis on the use of large scale tests to monitor students' progress toward meeting educational standards and hold schools and teachers accountable for this progress. At the same time, other educational trends, such as including more students with disabilities and more English language learners into general education classes, are making our classrooms more diverse than ever before.

Collectively, we have worked in education for nearly a century. We are familiar with the challenges that educators face in teaching academically, culturally, and linguistically diverse populations of students. We have worked in urban, suburban, and rural schools in 10 different states across the country. Each of us has experience in a variety of different educational contexts including elementary, middle, and high schools, and in university settings. We have served in a variety of roles, including general education teacher, special education teacher, reading specialist, consultant, administrator, teacher educator, and researcher. Throughout these varied experiences, we have found a common challenge—How do we appropriately respond to student diversity while maintaining high standards?

For teachers attempting to satisfy the seemingly contradictory needs of both standards-based reform and inclusion, several questions are often raised. Some of these questions are—"How can I effectively address the needs of such a diverse range of students?" or "How can I assist my students in reaching the established standards when many of them are so far behind or different from the students I am used to teaching?" or "How can I honor each student's individual differences and work toward the same goals for all students?" Herein lies the challenge—How can teachers in diverse classrooms deliver instruction that will help all students reach established standards? This book responds to that challenge by providing a framework for teaching and learning that gives concrete tools and strategies to accomplish this goal.

In working with teachers in a variety of school districts, we have found that teachers feel pulled in many different directions. On the one hand, they are asked to respect and accommodate individual student's learning differences. But then they are held accountable for teaching all students the same set of standards. In order to accomplish this goal, teachers are mandated to implement an ever increasing array of educational practices. Too often, there is no attempt to demonstrate how these practices are related or support each other. Teachers also don't know how these goals fit together in the big picture to accomplish the overall objective of maximizing educational outcomes for all students.

To address this challenge, we have drawn from an eclectic body of research and our own teaching experiences to develop a framework that helps to integrate multiple instructional approaches designed to meet the needs of diverse learners. The purpose of this book is to share this framework and to provide educators with concrete strategies for implementing standards-based instruction in diverse and inclusive classrooms. This book will provide a conceptual framework to address Ms. Noble's query—"What is the best way to accommodate each student's individual learning needs while simultaneously teaching the same standards for everyone?"

INTRODUCTION
Teaching in Diverse, Standards-Based Classrooms

Today's schools are becoming increasingly diverse. Many teachers find that their classrooms are populated by English language learners, gifted students, students with disabilities, and students who are culturally diverse. Nearly half of all students in U.S. public schools (42 percent) are students of color, approximately 20 percent of students speak a language other than English at home, and approximately 14 percent of students have an identified disability (U.S. Department of Education, 2007a). Approximately half of the students who have an identified disability spend 80 percent of their school day in general education classrooms (U.S. Department of Education, 2007b). To add to this diversity, approximately 12 percent of students in public schools are labeled as gifted and talented (Friend, 2007). Like their peers with disabilities, gifted and talented students also are integrated into general education classrooms. All of these differences make teaching more interesting and exciting as well as more complex.

Educational Trends That Affect Teaching

Standards-Based Reform

Despite a wide range of student differences—or perhaps because of it— there is an increased emphasis to have all students reach the same academic goals and standards. Some education experts have referred to this movement as "standards-based reform." Many advocates of standards-based reform have argued that expectations for students have been too low, especially for students with disabilities and students from minority groups and lower socioeconomic classes. This perception has led to the idea that whatever standards or educational goals are set should be uniformly applied to the vast majority of students and particular attention should be given to historically underperforming groups. This shift in thinking has been a challenge for educators. Despite the challenges with standard-based reform, this movement holds many promises, such as

- Helping educators focus on critical knowledge and skills.
- Enhancing the coherence and continuity of instruction by eliminating what some educators have viewed as a chaotic patchwork of curricula that may vary from teacher to teacher or from school to school.
- Addressing the soft bigotry associated with lower expectations for poor and minority students.
- Serving as a catalyst to promote collaboration between teachers in general education, special education, ESL, and bilingual education. Standards-based reform also helps educators share responsibility and accountability for the progress of all students, including students with disabilities and students from diverse backgrounds.

Inclusion

As attention increases to ensure that all learners reach common standards, there is also more attention focused on integrating students with disabilities into general education classrooms. Some experts have referred to this movement as "inclusion." It is important to note, however, that the physical placement of students with disabilities in general education classes is not an end in and of itself, but rather a means to an end. The power of inclusion lies in how educators respond to individual differences. While standards-based reform calls for convergence in terms of learning outcomes, inclusion calls for divergence in terms of the strategies used in teaching. When inclusion is considered alongside standards-based reform, it would appear that teachers are being called upon to produce greater similarity in learning outcomes despite greater diversity in student populations. For teachers who are attempting to manage the tension between standards-based reform and inclusion, there are still many challenges. Inclusion provides many opportunities for educators, such as

- **Enhancing access to general education curriculum for students with disabilities.** Greater academic gains have been associated with general education placement for students with disabilities (Waldron & McLeskey, 1998). This enhanced access to a general education curriculum should include Universal Design for Learning (UDL) principles and materials for students with difficulties reading and understanding print that meet the National Instructional Materials Accessibility Standard (NIMAS). This support is particularly important in a standards-based context because most students with disabilities will be held to the same educational standards as their peers without disabilities.
- **Providing greater opportunities for students with disabilities to learn socially appropriate behaviors through interaction with their peers without disabilities.** For example, when segregated in separate settings, students who have emotional or behavioral disorders are exposed only to other students who have similar disorders. This practice limits their opportunities to see appropriate behaviors and diminishes their inclination to conform to these behaviors through the dynamics of peer pressure.
- **Preparing students with and without disabilities for the real world.** As adults, students will be exposed to a wide range of human variance, including individuals with disabilities. By providing opportunities for all students to have interactions with students with disabilities during their educational experience, the groundwork will be laid for these students to embrace all individuals with disabilities throughout their lives.

Cultural and Linguistic Diversity

Of course, disability status reflects only one aspect of human diversity. Factors such as race, ethnicity, class, gender, and language also contribute to the classroom mosaic and may influence the cultural characteristics that students bring. Given the pervasive manner in which culture influences thought and behavior, it is not hard to imagine that it plays a significant role in the learning process. In fact, almost every aspect of the teaching and learning process is culturally influenced, such as attitudes about what is important to learn and decisions about how learning is best accomplished and assessed. While student diversity provides a rich educational resource, it also adds to the complexity of teaching in a standards-based context. Nevertheless, there are many opportunities that cultural diversity provides, such as

- **Providing opportunities for all students to learn from other students who are different.** Cultural diversity gives students a chance to learn about different languages, customs, and worldviews.
- **Reducing ignorance that comes from lack of exposure.** Oftentimes, when students only interact with persons who share the same background, they become blind to other ways of seeing and doing things. This cultural isolation frequently works to their disadvantage.
- **Providing opportunities for all students to develop cross-cultural competence.** Through everyday activities in diverse school settings, students are challenged to find ways of interacting effectively with students who are culturally different. In so doing, they develop important skills in cross-cultural competence.
- **Preparing students for the real world.** Similar to inclusion, giving students opportunities to interact with diverse individuals in their school experiences better prepares them to do so as adults in the workplace.

Integrating standards-based reform, including students with disabilities, and teaching more students from culturally and linguistically diverse backgrounds combine to create the perfect educational storm. How do all of these trends fit together? In some regards, these trends may seem to reflect incompatible ideas. On one hand, these movements were created to provide the same standards for all learners; but each reform mandates respect for each student's individual differences. The next section addresses these tensions.

Can Inclusion Really Work in Diverse, Standards-Based Classrooms?

Despite the fact that it is not always possible to get all students to exactly the same point in the curriculum at exactly the same time, it is feasible to move most students through the curriculum toward established standards. Although the concepts of inclusion and teaching for cultural and linguistic diversity often seem to conflict with standards-based reform, these ideas actually work together.

As is shown in Figure I.1, the overarching goals of standards-based reform, inclusion, and teaching for cultural and linguistic diversity are the same—to enhance the educational outcomes for all students. For example, standards-based reform emphasizes the need to support all students in reaching rigorous standards. Students with disabilities and students with culturally and linguistically diverse backgrounds have historically been among the most vulnerable to diminished educational outcomes as a result of low expectations. The reality is that the vast majority of students with disabilities and students from culturally and linguistically diverse backgrounds do not have severe cognitive deficits. These students have the ability to succeed academically in the

FIGURE I.1
Current Movements in Education

	Standards-Based Reform	Inclusion	Education for Diversity
Overarching Goal	• Enhance educational outcomes for all students	• Enhance educational outcomes for all students	• Enhance educational outcomes for all students
Basic Tenet	• Educational outcomes can be enhanced by setting rigorous standards, teaching to those standards, and assessing progress toward accomplishing those standards	• Educational outcomes can be enhanced by maximizing opportunities for students with and without disabilities to be educated together	• Educational outcomes can be enhanced by embracing student diversity
Associated Instructional Practices	• Curriculum is aligned with standards • Uses large-scale assessments	• Differentiated instruction • Universal design	• Multicultural education • Sheltered instruction

inclusive classroom. While raising standards is not the same thing as raising expectations, some educators feel that the accountability assessments associated with standards-based reform will force the issue of higher expectations. It is possible that we will have to change our behaviors and adjust our attitudes and expectations. For example, a teacher may not initially believe in a student's ability to meet a certain standard; however, that teacher will still earnestly work with that student because he or she will encounter that same standard on an accountability assessment in the future. Despite the teacher's initial doubts, the student may master the standard in question. This student's achievement will make it possible for that teacher to see potential in other students with similar characteristics. Without the standards and accountability assessment processes, this teacher may never have given this student the opportunity to master the standard in question. The core idea of not underestimating students' abilities is implicit in standards-based reform and holds particular importance in the education of diverse students.

The metaphor of all boats rising or sinking together is often used when describing approaches to standards-based reform, such as the No Child Left Behind Act. For example, in order for a school to achieve adequate yearly progress (AYP), all student subgroups, including English language learners, students with disabilities, and students from minority groups, must make adequate yearly progress. The progress of the group as a whole cannot mask the lack of development of designated subgroups. To extend the nautical metaphor, we can't ignore a hole in our neighbor's end of the boat and still expect to have our end remain dry. Special education students and other historically marginalized groups cannot be sent to the trailer and be forgotten.

The goal of helping all students meet rigorous standards can only be attained by attending to the needs of the most vulnerable students—students with disabilities and students from culturally and linguistically diverse backgrounds. The ideas embodied in movements such as inclusion and teaching for cultural and linguistic diversity provide this needed attention. Additionally, while standards-based reform is largely silent on the issue of instructional methodology, the inclusion and teaching for cultural and linguistic diversity movements infuse instructional approaches that maximize opportunities for all students to learn from their diverse peers. These approaches include differentiated instruction, universal design, sheltered instruction, and multi-cultural education.

Instructional Approaches That Support Inclusion in Diverse, Standards-Based Classrooms

Differentiated Instruction

Without the supporting pedagogy, inclusion in diverse, standards-based classrooms could not be successful. Differentiated instruction is an example of a supporting instructional approach that embraces the needs of academically diverse populations of students, in particular students who are gifted or who have disabilities. Differentiated instruction involves creating multiple paths to learning for diverse students (Tomlinson, 1999). Instruction can be differentiated in a variety of ways, such as tailoring content to an individual student's needs, modifying instructional methods to address student learning characteristics more appropriately, or adjusting learning products or assignments based on a student's skill and ability levels.

Universal Design for Learning

Universal design is an instructional approach that gives particular attention to students who have physical, sensory, and cognitive disabilities. Like differentiated instruction, universal design embraces the idea that instruction should be designed from the beginning with students' diverse needs in mind. Universal design supports the thought that educators should not have to retrofit lessons for students with exceptional needs after those lessons have already been created. According to Orkwis (1999), "Universal design implies a design of instructional materials and activities that allows learning goals to be attainable by individuals with wide differences in their abilities to see, hear, speak, move, read, write, understand English, attend, organize, engage, and remember" (p. 1). With universal design, it is important that learning activities provide multiple means of representation or modes of presentation (i.e., auditory, visual, and varying levels of complexity). Learning activities also must allow students to respond in various modes and should be designed to engage learners with varying interests and aptitudes. Often, educators use assistive technology to implement universal design to make instruction accessible for a broader array of students. Assistive technology refers to "any item, piece of equipment, or product system, whether acquired commercially off the shelf, modified, or customized, that is used to increase, maintain, or improve functional capabilities of a child with a disability" (U.S. Department of Education, 2004, 20 U.S.C. 1401 (a) (25)). Hence, low-tech devices such as pencil grips may be considered assistive technology as well as high-tech devices such as screen readers or electronic books. The principles of universal design are important to engineering classrooms that support diverse learners, including those students with physical, sensory, and cognitive disabilities (see Chapter 2 for an in-depth discussion on UDL).

Sheltered Instruction

Like differentiated instruction and universal design, sheltered instruction also embraces the needs of diverse learners, specifically English language learners. Echevarria, Vogt, and Short (2004) define sheltered instruction by using the following eight broad elements: (1) preparation, (2) building background, (3) comprehensible input, (4) strategies, (5) interaction, (6) practice and application, (7) lesson delivery, and (8) review and assessment. The preparation element suggests that teachers first identify lesson objectives aligned with state and local standards. The building background element requires that teachers link new content to students' background experiences and helps students focus on unfamiliar vocabulary. With the comprehensible input element, as the name implies, teachers use controlled vocabulary, sentence structure, and visuals and gestures to facilitate students' comprehension. The strategies element refers to teaching students different approaches for organizing and retaining information associated with effective learning. The interaction element shows teachers how to structure opportunities for students to interact with their peers in the learning process. The interaction phase leads to the practice and application element, which requires teachers to provide frequent opportunities for students to practice new language skills in context. The lesson delivery element illustrates how teachers can appropriately pace the lesson and provide for active engagement. The review and assessment element focuses on establishing standards and including language-based and content-based evaluations. All of these elements are important in designing classroom instruction that embraces the needs of English language learners.

Multicultural Education

Multicultural education is another approach that is important in today's diverse, standards-based classrooms. As the name implies, multicultural education addresses the needs of culturally diverse populations of students. Banks (2001) defined this approach with the following five major dimensions: (1) content integration, (2) the knowledge construction process, (3) bias reduction, (4) empowering school culture, and (5) equity pedagogy. Content integration implies that curricula should include content about diverse populations and present information from diverse points of view. The knowledge construction process focuses on the extent to which teachers explore the influences of culture with students. This process includes exploring how knowledge is constructed and how attitudes are formed in regards to what constitutes valuable or important knowledge. Bias reduction refers to activities that are designed to examine and reduce bias in attitudes. Building an empowering school culture eradicates systemic factors such as the negative effects of tracking practices on diverse groups of students. Equity pedagogy helps teachers use instructional strategies that embrace the learning characteristics and cognitive styles of diverse populations. Multicultural education supports educators in enhancing the educational experiences of all learners, including students from culturally diverse backgrounds.

Together, differentiated instruction, sheltered instruction, universal design, and multicultural education address the broad array of students in today's classrooms. By using these approaches, teachers have the pedagogical tools they need to teach standards in diverse, inclusive classrooms.

MMECCA: A Framework for Success

As you read the descriptions of the instructional approaches, you probably noticed that there was some similarity in the strategies used for each. For example, encouraging teachers to vary how they present content to students is a common theme for all of the instructional approaches. This overlap suggests

FIGURE I.2
Elements of Instruction in Inclusive, Standards-Based Classrooms

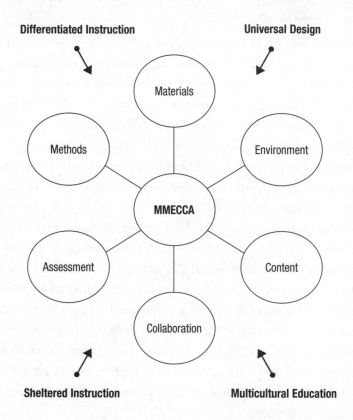

that teachers need not have a separate repertoire of strategies for each aspect of student diversity. Rather, it may be more helpful to consider implications of student diversity on the critical elements of instruction. Combining instruction with an awareness of student diversity is the theme of this book. The following chapters will focus on the MMECCA framework which is composed of six critical elements of instruction that must be addressed to appropriately respond to student diversity in standards-based classrooms. As shown in Figure I.2, the MMECCA framework helps to integrate the four instructional approaches associated with teaching diverse populations that were discussed in the previous section. This MMECCA framework is composed of the following elements:

- **Methods of Instruction.** This element shows the strategies and techniques that are employed during instruction. This is the "how" through which instruction is accomplished.
- **Materials of Instruction.** This element pertains to the tangible items that are used to support instruction. This is the "with what" through which instruction is accomplished.
- **Environment of Instruction.** This element focuses on the physical environment of the classroom, behavior management, and general classroom ethos. This is the "where" of instruction or the instructional context in which learning will occur.
- **Content of Instruction.** This element details what is being taught to students. It addresses curricular issues related to what students should know and be able to do. This is the "what" of the learning process or the knowledge, facts, and understandings that are the essence of teaching and learning.
- **Collaboration for Instruction.** This element pertains to how educators should work together in delivering instruction to diverse populations. It includes educational practices such as collaborative problem solving and co-teaching. This element also addresses how educators and parents should work together. This is the "it takes a village" element of instruction.
- **Assessment in Instruction.** Finally, this element focuses on the assessment process that begins and ends the instructional cycle. It includes informal, teacher-made assessments, as well as large-scale standardized tests. This is the "how do we know what students need and what they know?" element of the instructional process.

This framework has been field tested in 50 diverse, standards-based classrooms. Participating teachers were trained to use the MMECCA framework during a three-month period. They developed lessons using this framework, taught the lessons, and then evaluated the outcomes. Participating teachers reported that using the MMECCA framework enhanced their ability to design lessons that met the educational needs of their diverse students. For example, one teacher said, "Learning about the MMECCA framework in-depth has really helped me in working with special needs students." Student work samples taken from the lessons were evaluated based on how they mastered the standards targeted in the lesson. These student work samples and the teachers' reflections supported the teachers' reported growth in the area of teaching in inclusive, standards-based classrooms (Voltz, 2006).

The remaining chapters of this book will address each element of the MMECCA framework in-depth. Suggestions on integrating these ideas into your instruction will be provided in each chapter. We will follow elementary, middle, and high school teachers as they examine these six elements of their instruction. Through the lens of the instructional models associated with inclusion and teaching for cultural and linguistic diversity, each of the elements from the MMECCA framework will be explored and concrete strategies and illustrative examples will be provided to show how inclusion in diverse, standard-based classrooms can work for YOU!

Resources for MMECCA Framework

BOOKS

Banks, J. A., & Banks, C. M. (2009). *Multicultural education: Issues and perspectives.* Indianapolis, IN: Wiley.

Conklin, W., & Frei, S. (2007). *Differentiating the curriculum for gifted learners.* Huntington Beach, CA: Shell Education.

Council for Exceptional Children. (2005). *Universal design for learning.* Alexandria, VA: Author.

Echevarria, J., & Graves, A. (2010). *Sheltered content instruction: Teaching English language learners with diverse abilities.* Boston: Allyn and Bacon.

Gregory, G. H., & Chapman, C. M. (2006). *Differentiated instructional strategies: One size doesn't fit all.* Thousand Oaks, CA: Corwin.

Rose, D. H., & Mayer, R. (2002). *Teaching every student in the digital age: Universal design for learning.* Alexandria, VA: ASCD.

Tomlinson, C. (2004). *How to differentiate instruction in mixed ability classrooms.* Alexandria, VA: ASCD.

1

Gathering and Using the Best Methods for Instruction

As educators, we face many challenges as we decide which methods are best for organizing and delivering instruction to diverse populations of students. The strategies and methods we use play a critical role in developing successful instruction in diverse classrooms. How we decide to teach is important for all learners, especially for students with disabilities, students from culturally or linguistically diverse backgrounds, and students who are different in other educationally relevant ways. For these students, it is especially important that we maximize their opportunities to learn by using instructional strategies that correspond to their unique learning needs. In this chapter, we will discuss the first element of the MMECCA framework, the **METHODS** of instruction.

Examples of Powerful Instructional Methods

The key to success in diverse classrooms is selecting and implementing powerful instructional methods that simultaneously address a variety of different learning needs. Some of the methods that have worked well within our classrooms include multiple intelligences, cooperative learning, tiered lessons, learning centers, and graphic organizers. Figure 1.1 shows how each of

FIGURE 1.1
Powerful Instructional Models and Approaches

	INSTRUCTIONAL APPROACHES			
INSTRUCTIONAL METHODS	**Differentiated Instruction**	**Universal Design**	**Sheltered Instruction**	**Multicultural Education**
Multiple Intelligences	Encourages process and product differentiation	Allows for multiple means of receiving and demonstrating knowledge	Encourages the use of visual cues to supplement language	Encourages respect for diversity in learning styles
Cooperative Learning	Uses differentiation in role assignment	Capitalizes on learners' heterogeneity	Supports English language learners through peer mediation	Encourages respect for cooperative learning styles
Tiered Lessons	Encourages process and product differentiation	Allows for multiple means of receiving and demonstrating knowledge	Provides a vehicle for differentiating language levels	Encourages respect for diversity in learning styles
Learning Centers	Encourages process and product differentiation	Allows for multiple means of receiving and demonstrating knowledge	Provides a vehicle for differentiating language levels	Encourages respect for diversity in learning styles
Graphic Organizers	Provides a vehicle for scaffolding instruction	Provides a vehicle for scaffolding instruction	Provides a vehicle for scaffolding instruction	Embraces diverse learners' needs

these methods reflects ideas associated with differentiated instruction, universal design, sheltered instruction, and multicultural education. The next section will describe each of these methods and provide specific examples from classroom scenarios.

Multiple Intelligences

The theory of multiple intelligences developed by Howard Gardner (1999), co-director of Harvard's Project Zero, is used extensively in educational settings. In essence, the theory states that we, as humans, have unlimited "bio-, neuron-, and psychological potential for knowing, for acquiring information, [and] for understanding" (Lazear, 2001, p. 202). According to Gardner

(1999), intelligences are the skills and abilities we need to solve problems, create effective products, or provide services that are valuable in one's culture.

Currently, Gardner has identified eight intelligences—(1) linguistic, (2) logical-mathematical, (3) musical-rhythmic, (4) visual-spatial, (5) bodily-kinesthetic, (6) interpersonal, (7) intrapersonal, and (8) naturalist. An additional intelligence, existentialist, has been cited by some (Kellough & Kellough, 2007), although Gardner has yet to confirm it as the ninth intelligence. We have included it for your consideration. Figure 1.2 lists each of the intelligences and shows the range of characteristic abilities and talents that students can have. Given what we know about the theory of multiple intelligences, we can see its potential for increasing success with all students, especially struggling learners (Zwiers, 2004). By using the theory of multiple intelligences, we can determine students' learning strengths based on how we present concepts and ideas in the classroom.

FIGURE 1.2
Definitions and Capacities for Multiple Intelligences

Intelligence	Definition	Capacity
Bodily-Kinesthetic	This person has the ability to move through space effectively, learns well with movement, and can imitate movements easily.	• Has improved body function • Has miming abilities • Has a keen mind-body connection • Can expand awareness through the body
Intrapersonal	This person understands his or her own ways of knowing and learning and is in tune with his or her own needs.	• Has keen mind concentration • Has awareness and can express different feelings • Has higher order thinking and reasoning
Interpersonal	This person reads others well, works well in groups, and interacts effectively with other people.	• Can create and maintain synergy • Can discern underlying intentions, behavior, and perceptions • Is tuned into others' perspectives • Knows how to work cooperatively • Is sensitive to others' moods, motives, and feelings • Can communicate verbally and nonverbally

(continued on next page)

FIGURE 1.2

Definitions and Capacities for Multiple Intelligences *(con't)*

Intelligence	Definition	Capacity
Verbal-Linguistic	This person manipulates words and language easily, understands what he or she reads, and enjoys verbal interactions.	• Understands the order and meaning of words • Can convince someone of a course of action • Can explain, teach, and learn from others • Has a sense of humor • Has a keen memory and recall
Logical-Mathematical	This person manipulates numbers and logic easily and understands the logical connections among concepts.	• Recognizes abstract patterns • Has the ability to reason inductively and deductively • Can discern relationships and connections • Can perform complex calculations • Has the ability to reason scientifically
Musical-Rhythmic	This person expresses him- or herself easily in rhythm and melody and sees patterns and music in all endeavors.	• Understands the structure of music • Understands schemas for hearing music • Is sensitive to sounds • Can create melodies and rhythms • Can sense qualities of a tone
Visual-Spatial	This person can see pleasing visual-spatial arrangements and has the ability to learn and express him or herself with visual arrangements, art, and beauty.	• Has accurate perceptions from different angles • Can recognize relationships between objects in space • Can create graphic representations • Can manipulate images • Can find his or her way through space • Forms mental images • Has an active imagination
Naturalist	This person values and cares for nature and living things and has the ability to classify species and grow natural things.	• Communes with nature • Cares for, tames, and interacts with living creatures • Is sensitive to nature's flora • Can recognize and classify species • Can grow things naturally
Existentialist	This person has the inclination to raise and explore questions about human existence and the meaning of life.	• Is a deep thinker • Is sensitive to spiritual issues

Multiple Intelligences Capacities Summary (p. 205) by D. Lazear, 2001, Upper Saddle River, NJ: Prentice Hall and *Multiple Intelligences in the Classroom* (pp. 6–7) by T. Armstrong, 2009, Alexandria, VA: ASCD. Adapted with permission.

Applying Multiple Intelligences in the Classroom

The following scenario shows how Ms. Smith uses the theory of multiple intelligences in her 10th grade English classroom at Meadow Brook High School. In this scenario we meet three of her students, Tranhi, Victor, and Jasmine.

Tranhi is 17 years old. She and her family moved to the United States from Vietnam six years ago. Both of her parents and her two sisters work long hours in a local nail salon. Her family speaks Vietnamese at home with a smattering of English. Tranhi is personable yet shy. Her favorite times of the school day are during choir practice and modern dance class. School is very challenging for her. She is able to understand her peers, but she is frustrated by her limited grasp of the specialized vocabulary in her academic classes.

Victor is 17 years old. He and his mother moved to the United States from the Ukraine last summer. His mother is trained as a nurse, but because of language difficulties and certification problems, she works as a nurse's assistant at the local hospital. In Victor's home, he is encouraged to speak English. He loves the sciences, math, and technology. He was an academically proficient student back in the Ukraine; however, he is currently struggling in his English and social studies classes because his English language skills are limited. He dreams of becoming an orthopedic surgeon.

Jasmine is a 16-year-old multiracial female student. Her father is a truck driver who travels away from home most of the time, and her mother works in the bakery at the local supermarket. Of all her classes, Jasmine enjoys English the best. For Jasmine, books have taken the place of friends. She does not have a peer group. Jasmine has the potential to be an excellent student in English class, but she prefers to just get by. School does not seem to be very important for Jasmine.

Ms. Smith has taught at Meadow Brook High School for 12 years. Meadow Brook is a suburban high school that has traditionally served a white, upper middle class population of students. Within the last few years, however, there has been an increase in the number of immigrant students who have enrolled in the school. Many of these students are English language learners and represent a range of different countries and languages. The religious diversity of the student population also has increased with the inclusion of students who are Buddhist, Muslim, Jewish, Christian, and many other faiths. Approximately 85 percent of the students are white, and the remaining students are African American, Asian, Indian, or Hispanic. With the increased emphasis on inclusion, more students with disabilities are also appearing in general education classrooms at Meadow Brook High School. Out of the 130 students that Ms. Smith teaches each day, 10 students have disabilities, which include learning disorders, mild mental retardation, emotional disturbance, speech impairment, and hearing loss.

Despite Meadow Brook's strong reputation for academic excellence, the unthinkable happened during the last year's assessment cycle—Meadow Brook failed to make adequate yearly progress (AYP) toward established standards. The school's failure to make AYP was based on low test scores from English language learners and students with disabilities. Ms. Smith began wondering why all this "standards stuff" had to hit at the same time that the staff was charged with moving forward on inclusion AND receiving more students from culturally and linguistically diverse backgrounds. Ms. Smith knows she will have to change her game plan to be more effective with these students, but she is not sure how to do it.

Ms. Smith is beginning a mini-unit on the 10th grade English standard related to naturalism. This literary movement is characterized by pessimistic determinism, which is distinguished by the belief that people have little or no control over their lives. She is excited about this unit because she believes that all of her students will be able to connect to this theme and relate it to their challenges as adolescents.

Before beginning the unit, Ms. Smith observed her students and gave them a brief survey to determine their strengths based on the theory of multiple intelligences. Based on her findings from Tranhi, Victor, and Jasmine's results, she identified appropriate learning activities for the unit that tap into each student's strengths.

As Ms. Smith uses techniques that reflect each of her students' intelligences, she also allows them to work in flexible groupings of pairs, triads, quads, small groups, and whole groups. She uses each student's strength as an entry point into the content. For Tranhi, Ms. Smith makes sure that there is a musical hook in the introduction of her content. She considers allowing the class to listen to an appropriate selection by Wagner or a Vietnamese selection that creates a mood of uncertainty and dread. For Victor, she creates a problematic perspective that involves an athlete with an artificial leg wishing to play in the World Cup games. Finally, for Jasmine, Ms. Smith links popular culture to the concept of naturalism. She brings in various photographs of young pop idols and asks Jasmine to identify the physical characteristics that help or hurt their careers. After a small-group discussion period, Ms. Smith brings all the students together, asks them to identify the common thread for all of the scenarios, and links their thinking to the planned unit. Once the students' interests are piqued, Ms. Smith continues her plans to integrate the theory of multiple intelligences into her instructional unit. She understands that while connecting students' learning to their dominant intelligences is important, students also need to experience other ways of receiving information so that they can have opportunities to enhance their less dominant intelligences. By weaving different intelligences into her instructional methods, she exposes all of her students to diverse ways of learning.

Getting the Most Out of the Theory of Multiple Intelligences

As you begin this approach, it is helpful to use assessment strategies such as student interviews, questionnaires, or observations to discover your students' strongest intelligences. Examples of these assessment tools are discussed further in Chapter 6. You can begin this assessment process by first targeting the students who struggle most and then moving on to other students as time allows. For your professional growth, use the grid in Figure 1.3 to analyze your current teaching methods with respect to the theory of multiple intelligences and see which intelligences you use the most. You could also use this grid to reflect on your last week of instruction and indicate how you utilized each of the intelligences. In many instances, we tend to emphasize verbal-linguistic and logical-mathematic skills. If you find that this is the case for you, gradually incorporate other intelligences into your repertoire. Begin with the intelligences that are strongest for your students.

FIGURE 1.3
Multiple Intelligences Instructional Grid

	Monday	Tuesday	Wednesday	Thursday	Friday
Verbal-Linguistic	Addressed? How?	Addressed? How?	Addressed? How?	Addressed? How?	Addressed? How?
Logical-Mathematical	Addressed? How?	Addressed? How?	Addressed? How?	Addressed? How?	Addressed? How?
Visual-Spatial	Addressed? How?	Addressed? How?	Addressed? How?	Addressed? How?	Addressed? How?
Bodily-Kinesthetic	Addressed? How?	Addressed? How?	Addressed? How?	Addressed? How?	Addressed? How?
Musical-Rhythmic	Addressed? How?	Addressed? How?	Addressed? How?	Addressed? How?	Addressed? How?
Interpersonal	Addressed? How?	Addressed? How?	Addressed? How?	Addressed? How?	Addressed? How?
Intrapersonal	Addressed? How?	Addressed? How?	Addressed? How?	Addressed? How?	Addressed? How?
Naturalist	Addressed? How?	Addressed? How?	Addressed? How?	Addressed? How?	Addressed? How?
Existentialist	Addressed? How?	Addressed? How?	Addressed? How?	Addressed? How?	Addressed? How?

As you move forward with the theory of multiple intelligences, it is important to keep the following strategies in mind:

- **It is not necessary to address all of the intelligences in every lesson.** However, it is appropriate to strive to address each intelligence at least once a week during instruction.
- **It is important to make sure that how you address each intelligence is not superficial or tangential to the learning at hand.** For example, telling students to stand while they read is not a strong example of incorporating bodily-kinesthetic learning opportunities. The act of

standing does not help the student learn how to read. If you are teaching a unit on the circulatory system, a better example of a bodily-kinesthetic activity would be to allow students to simulate walking through a human heart. Students can create a very large diagram that shows the various chambers of the heart. This diagram can be placed on the floor. Small groups of students can then walk through the chambers in the diagram to gain a greater understanding of how the blood flows through the heart. This activity would be more beneficial to students because movement is used to reinforce the concept being taught.

- **Remind students that the theory of multiple intelligences helps them focus on "How you are smart," not "How smart are you?"** Everyone has relative strengths and weaknesses.
- **It is important for all students to have opportunities to work through an intelligence that is not their current strength.** For some students, their lack of exposure to a specific intelligence could be the cause of weakness. For example, if a student never had an opportunity to participate in musical-rhythmic activities, he or she probably will not be strong in this area due to lack of exposure rather than any intrinsic weakness.
- **When encouraging a student to work through an intelligence that he or she does not prefer, select content that is somewhat familiar.** It would be difficult for a student to learn new content or skills through an unfamiliar intelligence.

Cooperative Learning

Cooperative learning is an instructional format used in heterogeneous learning environments. This instructional method is often confused with the concept of "group work" or the idea that students simply work together to accomplish a task. Cooperative learning is a specific type of group work that has the following defining elements:

- **Positive interdependence.** Learning activities are structured in such a way that students are required to depend on one another to successfully accomplish a task. The success of the whole group depends upon the performance of each group member.

- **Face-to-face interaction.** Each activity requires extended time for students to interact directly with each other.
- **Individual accountability.** Each person can be evaluated and held accountable for some specific element of the task.
- **Social skill development.** In addition to the academic content being taught, social skills are incorporated into students' learning.
- **Evaluation.** This step includes evaluating academic and social learning outcomes and how the group functions. (Johnson & Johnson, 1989)

Implementing the Defining Elements of Cooperative Learning

There are a variety of techniques that teachers can use to incorporate the defining elements of cooperative learning into group activities. You can assign specific roles to each student in the group, such as scribe, reader, encourager, or illustrator. Students then have the opportunity to rotate through these roles during different cooperative learning activities. Assigning roles helps students develop positive interdependence and individual accountability.

A number of specific cooperative learning formats can be used to facilitate face-to-face interaction, such as

- **Group Projects.** In the group projects format, each group is assigned to a specific task and each group member has a specific role (Sharan et al., 1984). Each role is essential to the overall success of the project.
- **Jigsaw.** Through the jigsaw format, students work first in "expert teams" to learn content about different topics in-depth and then teach it to other students. Next, the teams are reconfigured so that one member of each expert team forms a second round of groups. Each member of the reconfigured groups is then responsible for sharing with new group members the content that they mastered in the expert team (Slavin, 1994). For example, a social studies teacher decides that her students will focus on a unit about the branches of government. One expert team may focus on the legislative branch, another on the judicial branch, and a third on the executive branch. When the teams are reconfigured, one member of each expert group forms a second round of teams. These teams then work together to teach one another how the three branches of government function.

- **Student Teams Achievement Divisions.** A teacher gives each of her students a pre-test on selected content. Then, students form groups and assist one another in studying for a quiz on the content. Next, the teacher gives another round of individual quizzes, and each student earns points for the team based on his or her improvement from the pre-test (Slavin, 1994).

These formats provide structured face-to-face interaction among students and help facilitate positive interdependence. For example, in the jigsaw format, students must depend on fellow team members to accurately present the content they learn in expert teams. Students also use these same interdependence skills in the student teams achievement divisions format when they are required to coach one another in learning selected content. Individual accountability is important in cooperative learning because students are responsible for specific content. Finally, teachers can also evaluate academic content through each of these models.

Cooperative learning formats provide a natural laboratory for developing social skills. Social skills such as using names, communicating ideas and questions, taking turns, disagreeing amicably, and encouraging others are important skills that can be reinforced within the context of cooperative learning. Prior to beginning a cooperative learning activity, it may be helpful to do mini-lessons with your students around these skills. For example, if you have observed that your students have difficulty disagreeing amicably, then you might highlight this skill in a mini-lesson. Before the activity, you may want to discuss the fact that reasonable people sometimes disagree, and it's OK. What you do want to emphasize is that it is not OK to make personal attacks. You may decide to follow this brief discussion with role-playing activities that show appropriate and inappropriate ways to disagree with team members. This activity will allow students to practice this skill within the context of the cooperative learning activity.

Evaluation is another critical element of cooperative learning that can be incorporated into your lessons in a variety of ways. You can use an observation checklist to evaluate your students' social skills (see Figure 1.4). Your checklist can include columns for each of the targeted social skills and rows for each student's name. As you observe your students, you can record appropriate or inappropriate behaviors for each item on an individual basis. You can modify this form by using different skill lists for different sets of students. Additionally, peer evaluation forms can be used to supplement teacher evaluations (see Figure 1.5).

FIGURE 1.4
Cooperative Learning Observation Checklist

	Uses verbal encouragement	Contributes to group discussions	Shares materials	Is able to disagree amicably	Practices appropriate turn taking
Derrick					
Maria					
Shalandra					
LaMont					
John					
Lisa					

FIGURE 1.5
Cooperative Learning Peer Evaluation Form

Please rate yourself and each of your team members in each area using the following scale.

1—Poor 2—OK 3—Very Good

	Helped the group complete the activity	Shared materials	Encouraged group members
Derrick			
Maria			
Shalandra			
LaMont			

Applying Cooperative Learning in the Classroom

The following scenario shows an application of cooperative learning in Mr. Jones's 6th grade science class at West End Middle School. In this scenario, we meet four students from his class, Derrick, Maria, Shalandra, and LaMont.

Derrick is a 13-year-old African American male. He lives with his grandmother and two older siblings. He enjoys social studies and learning about and working with other people. He struggles with literacy and often needs concepts repeated several times before he grasps them.

Maria is 11 years old. Her family moved to the United States from Mexico three years ago. She is an only child and lives with her parents who co-own a small restaurant in the community. Spanish is the primary language spoken in her home. Maria excels in mathematics and enjoys puzzles, but she struggles with her English literacy skills.

Shalandra is a 12-year-old African American female. She lives with her father and her younger brother. Her father is a janitor at a local department store. Her mother died when she was 5 years old. Shalandra is an avid reader and enjoys creative writing. She is socially mature for her age and sometimes seems aloof and uninterested in interacting with her peers. She prefers to work alone.

LaMont is an 11-year-old African American male. He lives with his mother and two older sisters. La Mont's mother is unemployed. He is an excellent artist who can draw detailed and lifelike pictures. Despite his obvious intelligence, LaMont completes very few assignments and shows little interest in school. He can be noncompliant and seems angry most of the time. If he is pressured to do something that he doesn't want to do, he becomes volatile and physically aggressive. Because of these behaviors, LaMont has been identified as emotionally disturbed.

Mr. Jones is in his first year of teaching at West End Middle School, and he is excited to begin his new career. West End Middle School has been described as a "hard to staff" school in the inner city and has suffered from high teacher attrition rates. There are high transiency rates among students as well. Seventy five percent of the student population is African

American and 23 percent of the students are Hispanic, many of whom are English language learners. Eighty nine percent of the students receive free or reduced-priced lunches. Mr. Jones teaches approximately 150 students per day. Eighteen of these students have learning disabilities, mild mental retardation, emotional disturbances, speech impairments, or visual impairments.

Mr. Jones is energized by the diversity of the students in his classes; however, he is insecure about his ability to meet their needs. Additionally, he is concerned about the fact that West End Middle School has been designated as a "failing school" because of declining test scores. The school has never made adequate yearly progress for any year that students' performance has been tracked. Consequently, if students' test scores do not improve by the end of the school year, the school is in danger of closing. Mr. Jones wonders what he can do to enhance the achievement of his diverse group of students.

Mr. Jones has decided to use cooperative learning in his science classes. This learning format will embrace the diversity of his students and provide opportunities for them to support each other in learning challenging content. Although his students are 6th graders, Mr. Jones discovered that they have not been exposed to cooperative learning formats in their previous school experiences. He prepared them for cooperative learning by explaining what should and should not happen during cooperative learning, and he made time to reinforce these ideas through role-play activities.

After he prepared the class, Mr. Jones used a group project cooperative learning format. Since cooperative learning would be a new experience for his students, Mr. Jones used smaller groups of three to four students to reduce the complexity of interactions among team members. Mr. Jones assembled these groups with care. He wanted each group to be heterogeneous in terms of students' skill and ability levels, ethnicity, gender, and language characteristics. Mr. Jones also avoided placing students together who he knew would not work well with each other.

Mr. Jones planned a lesson based on the 6th grade standard related to exploring the earth's biomes. During this lesson students will learn about aquatic biomes, grasslands, deserts, chaparrals, taigas, and tundras. In order to meet this standard, students will need to be able to identify geographic factors in biomes (e.g., elevation, location, and climate) that cause diversity in flora and fauna. Mr. Jones's prior lessons in this unit included varied kinds of activities such as class discussion, hands-on activities, and videos focusing on the relationship of a biome's characteristics to the nature of plants and animals that live there. With this basic content in place, Mr. Jones is ready to begin the cooperative learning activity with his class.

Each group was assigned to research a different biome. All groups were required to do the following: (1) construct a three-dimensional model of their biome; (2) write a brief paper that defends their depiction of the biome and states how the characteristics of the biome affect the nature of the plants and animals that live there; and (3) present and explain their model to the class. Each group member has a specific role. The facilitator leads the group's discussion about how the model should be designed and defended, the scribe writes down the group's ideas for the report, the lead builder takes leadership for building the model, and the presenter explains the model to the class. Everyone in the group is responsible for participating in the group discussions, assisting with building the model, and gathering supporting evidence for the model. This last task involved using the science textbook and the Internet to find support for the design of the model. Students had access to one computer with Internet access and one computer with the CD-ROM of the textbook. Both computers included screen reading software.

Derrick, Maria, Shalandra, and LaMont were in a group for this activity. Maria served as the facilitator, Shalandra as the scribe, LaMont as the lead builder, and Derrick as the presenter. While each group worked on the assigned cooperative learning task, Mr. Jones checked each group to monitor progress, answer questions, reinforce appropriate behaviors, and troubleshoot. When Mr. Jones visited this specific group, he noticed that Shalandra seemed to be withdrawing from the group and writing the paper on her own. Mr. Jones decided to step in and guide the group in working together on deciding what should be included in the paper. He also queried individual group members to check their levels of understanding with respect to the concepts at hand. During a second visit with this group, Mr. Jones found that LaMont was really engaged in building the model, and he praised him discreetly on his efforts. During a third visit to the group, Mr. Jones found that the majority of the group had misunderstood an important concept, so he conducted a mini-lesson with the group on the topic.

After the cooperative learning lesson was completed, Mr. Jones evaluated the targeted academic learning. For the academic learning, Mr. Jones created a rubric to help him evaluate the models, the accompanying papers, and the presentations. He also developed a brief pencil and paper quiz. His goal was to determine which students mastered identifying the geographic factors in biomes that cause diversity in flora and fauna. Mr. Jones also assessed the targeted social skills for each student. Because of Shalandra's and LaMont's previous emotional difficulties, Mr. Jones decided to document how they worked during cooperative learning time.

Getting the Most Out of Cooperative Learning

As you implement cooperative learning in your classroom, begin by helping students develop their interpersonal skills. These skills include communicating ideas effectively, taking turns appropriately during discussions, remaining focused on the topic, sharing materials, and disagreeing amicably. If you or your students are new to cooperative learning, start by using smaller groups with two to four students that meet once a week. As you move forward, keep the following concepts in mind:

Do not attempt to cover all instruction using a cooperative learning format. Instruction should include individual, small-group, and whole-group formats.

Explicitly outline behavioral and learning expectations for students prior to beginning cooperative learning activities. For example, expectations regarding voice volume, specific roles in the group (e.g., scribe, lead builder), or final products (e.g., biome models) should be clearly explained to students. You can use a fishbowl technique and allow students to model these roles for their peers. In the fishbowl technique, one group of students performs a brief cooperative learning activity while the rest of the class watches. Afterward, the class discusses the groups' strengths and ways in which the group can improve based on the guidelines of cooperative learning.

Provide special support to students as needed to help them participate effectively in cooperative learning. For example, using a "talking wand" may be helpful for young or impulsive students. Students are required to wait until they receive the talking wand before they speak. Other students may need visual reminders or checklists that can include the following items:

- Am I following instructions?
- Am I using a quiet voice?
- Am I contributing to the group discussion?
- Am I listening to my group members?
- Am I staying focused on the task?

Remove students from cooperative learning activities if they cannot focus on the task or are distracting others. Teachers should be prepared with an alternate learning activity that focuses on the same content in an individual format to accommodate students when they are not able to function in a group.

Tiered Lessons

Tiered lessons allow teachers to present a given concept to students at multiple levels of complexity or through multiple learning styles. According to Adams and Pierce (2003), "A tiered lesson addresses a particular standard, key concept, and generalization, but allows several pathways for students to arrive at an understanding of these components" (p. 31). Adams and Pierce (2003) identified the following steps for implementing tiered lessons:

- **Identify the standard that you are targeting.** Determine the key concepts or big ideas that are inherent in this standard. What should all students know or be able to do relative to this standard?
- **Determine what students already know or can do.** Will some students need help gaining prerequisite skills? Have some students already mastered the basic concept?
- **Choose what lessons you will tier and how you will tier the content, process, or product.** For example, if you are teaching a lesson on measuring to the nearest half inch, you may find that some students in the class have not yet mastered this skill while other students have. You may decide to tier the content by having one group focus on measuring to

the nearest inch, another on measuring to the nearest half inch, and yet another on measuring to the nearest quarter inch. You could also tier the process or the method through which students will experience the lesson.

- **Determine how many tiers you will have and match students to the appropriate tiers.** You may decide to have as few as two tiers or as many as five tiers based on the learning needs of your class.

Applying Tiered Lessons in the Classroom

The following scenario shows a tiered lesson strategy in Ms. Wilson's 3rd grade classroom. In this scenario we meet three students from her class, Dorothy, Jim, and Juan.

Dorothy is a 9-year-old white female student. She lives with her mother and two younger siblings. Her mother works as a waitress at a local pizza parlor. Dorothy's favorite subjects are social studies, music, and art. She learns best when she is working with her hands or with others. She was identified as mildly mentally retarded as a 2nd grader and has very weak literacy and math skills.

Jim is an 8-year-old African American male student. He is an only child and lives with his parents, both of whom are educators in another school district. Jim's favorite subject is science and his least favorite subject is social studies. He can perform at very high levels and was recently identified as a gifted student. Jim enjoys puzzles and appears to be an analytical thinker. Although Jim is a very capable student, he does not always put forth his best effort. If the topic is not interesting to him, or if he deems an activity "stupid," he will not engage and can become a behavior problem.

Juan is 8 years old. His family moved to the United States from Mexico two years ago. He lives with his parents and three older siblings. Juan's mother works at a fast food restaurant and his father works at a construction site. Spanish is the primary language spoken in his home. Juan's favorite subject is math. He also enjoys sports and is a great artist. Juan often struggles to express his thoughts in English and understand abstract concepts and academic language. His literacy skills are very low.

During the 20 years that Ms. Wilson has taught at Southside Elementary School, she has witnessed increasing diversity in the student population. More than 40 percent of her students are African American, Hispanic, or Asian; 20 percent are English language learners and speak either Hmong or Spanish; and most students receive free or reduced-priced lunches. Ms. Wilson also serves two children who have learning disabilities; one child has mild mental retardation and the other has a behavior disorder. Additionally, there are two students who are identified as gifted in her class.

The instructional and behavior management strategies that Ms. Wilson used with success in the past no longer seem to be working. Adding to her frustration is the fact that Southside Elementary has now been labeled a "school in crisis" because of its failure to make adequate yearly progress. With this new designation, Ms. Wilson and her colleagues are under increasing pressure to ensure that all students reach established benchmarks at the same time that the needs of the student population have become increasingly diverse.

Ms. Wilson used a tiered format to design a lesson to address the 3rd grade social studies standard for identifying ways to prepare for natural disasters in the United States. She decided to focus on this standard during a lesson on tornado preparedness. Ms. Wilson began the lesson with a preview of related vocabulary. Next, general content regarding tornado preparedness was presented through a video and a class discussion. A local meteorologist visited the class to discuss tornados and safety precautions and brought in a model that simulated a mini-tornado in action.

After this whole-group presentation, Ms. Wilson tiered the remaining class activities based on different tiers and learning projects (see Figure 1.6). Juan and 19 other classmates were assigned to tier 1 and were required to design posters that illustrated each of the steps to take during a tornado. After designing the posters, students in this tier paired up with a peer to explain their posters. Dorothy and four other classmates were assigned to tier 2 and worked together as a team to develop and perform a skit that depicted the steps to take during a tornado. Jim and two other classmates were assigned to tier 3 and developed PowerPoint presentations that briefly outlined what causes tornados, what steps to take during a tornado, and what kinds of damage tornados can cause. To complete these activities, students in tier 3 were required to do Internet research on specified sites to learn more about the causes and consequences of tornados.

FIGURE 1.6
Sample Lesson Plan for Tiered Instruction

Grade: 3rd
Subject Matter: Social Studies
Concept: Tornado Preparedness
Standard: Identify ways to prepare for natural disasters in the United States.

	Content	Process	Product
Tier 1	• Steps to take during a tornado	• Design and explain posters to peers	• Create a poster that illustrates steps to take during a tornado
Tier 2	• Steps to take during a tornado	• Work together as a team to develop skit	• Perform a skit that depicts steps to take during a tornado
Tier 3	• Steps to take during a tornado • Explain causes of tornados • Explain kinds of damage tornados can cause	• Conduct Internet research on specified sites	• Develop PowerPoint presentations that outlines the content

Ms. Wilson knew that Dorothy learned best by doing an activity, therefore she assigned her to the group that developed a skit. Likewise, Ms. Wilson recognized that social studies was Jim's least favorite subject, so she found a way to link it with a science concept. She also designed a learning activity that challenged Jim and extended his learning about tornado preparedness. Finally, Ms. Wilson capitalized on Juan's artistic skills and circumvented his literacy limitations by assigning him to the tier that required students to illustrate the steps to take during a tornado.

Getting the Most Out of Tiered Lessons

As you get started with this approach, begin with two tiers for each lesson and then you can add as many as five tiers as you become more comfortable with this approach. As with other approaches, it is important to prepare students for using tiered lessons. Create a classroom climate where students understand that the assignments will be differentiated for each student based on their needs. Students should understand that "fair" means that everyone gets what they need and not everyone will get the same thing. Strategies for facilitating this kind of classroom environment can be found in Chapter 4.

Learning Centers

Learning centers are another powerful instructional method that can be used to support diverse groups of learners. These centers are described as places "where a variety of activities introduce, reinforce, and/or extend learning, often without the assistance of the classroom teacher" (Opitz, 1994, p. 13). Keep the following guidelines in mind as you design your learning centers:

- **Learning centers should be phased in gradually if students don't have prior experience using them.** Before center time begins, students need explicit instructions regarding behavioral and academic expectations. This discussion should focus on rules for appropriate behavior when working in the learning center (e.g., using soft voices when talking and sharing materials), as well as the learning tasks that should be completed. Initially, students should only go to one center for a short period during this time. After students use the center, give them a "debriefing" that includes feedback about how well behavioral and academic expectations were met. As students become more familiar with learning centers, you can phase in more complex or lengthy center formats. Likewise, pre- and post-discussions regarding the learning center process can become more abbreviated.
- **In general, learning center activities should focus on material that students already know.** If students are working independently in the learning centers, they will need to have some familiarity with both the content and format of activities. This guideline would not apply if the teacher is stationed at one of the learning centers.
- **All materials that students will need to complete the required activities should be located in or near the center.** Providing easy access to all materials will reduce the need for students to stray away from the physical location of the center.

- **Center activities should be novel and engaging.** This appeal will serve as intrinsic motivation for students to complete the task at hand.
- **A system of accountability should be inherent in the center activity.** Students need to feel that there is an expected outcome for center activities and that they will be held responsible for this outcome. For example, in one center students may be expected to complete word puzzles. At the end of center time, students should submit a completed word puzzle to the teacher. This accountability reinforces the idea to students that while center time may be fun, productivity is still expected.

Learning centers can be implemented in a variety of ways. In some cases, students do not rotate among centers but remain at assigned centers for 25 to 45 minutes at a time. In this case, differentiation occurs within centers rather than between them. For example, in a high school English class with diverse students, several learning centers are set up to focus on punctuation. Four centers are set up for end punctuation, comma usage, quotations, and colons and semicolons. Students work in the same center during center time based on their punctuation needs. The teacher then visits each station to do a mini-lesson.

In other learning centers, students have the opportunity to visit multiple centers during each period. When learning centers are used in this way, students usually rotate through three to five centers and stay at each for 15 to 25 minutes. Activities in each center are then differentiated to meet the needs of diverse students.

Applying Learning Centers in the Classroom

The following scenario shows a learning center strategy from Ms. Wilson's 3rd grade classroom. In this scenario, we meet up with Dorothy, Jim, and Juan again and see how they interact with a learning center lesson plan.

Ms. Wilson frequently uses learning centers during the 90-minute math block in her class. Because many of her students have short attention spans, Ms. Wilson likes to give them frequent opportunities to shift activities and move around the room. Consequently, when Ms. Wilson uses learning centers, she often has students rotate among them in 15-minute intervals. Although her students are familiar with this format, Ms. Wilson still briefly reviews center activities and reminds students of behavioral expectations before they begin their work. She uses pictures and other graphics to support her explanations. During center activities, Ms. Wilson moves between each center to monitor students' work and answer questions as they arise.

Because of the diversity of the students in her class, Ms. Wilson differentiates activities within each learning center. She uses a color-coding system to cue students to the activities they need to complete. For example, some students may work on "red dot" activities while others work on "blue dot" or "yellow dot" activities.

Ms. Wilson designed a series of learning centers to reinforce skills related to the 3rd grade math standard for solving addition, subtraction, and word problems using two- and three-digit numbers with and without regrouping. During the first rotation, Dorothy, Jim, Juan, and their classmates visited center 1 which was designed to help them practice problem solving in math. In this center, Dorothy, Juan, and one other classmate worked at a bank of three computers. Juan's computer was loaded with software featuring subtraction word problems that were read aloud in Spanish into his earphones. These were single-step word problems that involved two-digit addition with regrouping. The software saved a record of Juan's performance for Ms. Wilson's review. Dorothy and another classmate worked at the other two computers which were loaded with software featuring basic math facts that were read aloud (e.g., "I had three pencils and found two more. How many do I have in all?"). These problems were accompanied with animated graphics that illustrated the problems. Jim and three other classmates worked on task cards featuring multi-step word problems involving three-digit subtraction with regrouping.

Center 2 was designed to reinforce basic facts. In this center, Dorothy and one other classmate were assigned to create a visual representation of several addition facts by gluing the indicated number of uncooked macaroni pieces underneath each problem. Initially, prompts such as __ __ __ + __ __ = __ __ __ __ __ were used to indicate where each piece of macaroni should be placed. In the same center, Juan and four other classmates worked with speed drills on subtraction facts. Jim and one other classmate did not work at this center because both students had already exceeded benchmarks on speed drills in both addition and subtraction facts. Instead, these two students remained at the problem-solving center and worked on making multi-step subtraction problems that were to be included in a word problem book for the entire class.

Center 3 focused on helping students develop accuracy with two- and three-digit addition and subtraction algorithms involving regrouping. Juan and three classmates worked on "mystery person" worksheets in which the correct answers were coded to letters that spelled out the name of a famous African American mathematician. These problems involved two-digit subtraction with regrouping. Jim and two other classmates worked on similar worksheets involving three-digit subtraction with regrouping. Dorothy and one other classmate did not participate in this center because its focus was not developmentally appropriate for them. Instead, both students remained at center 2 and continued to work on macaroni math facts.

Center 4 involved three game boards. Dorothy and one other classmate played one of these games together. This game included red problem cards with visual prompts. The cards featured problems such as $4 + 1 = \_\_$. With the correct answer, each player rolled the dice and advanced their playing piece on the board based on number indicated. Each player recorded the problems that they missed on a separate sheet. Juan and three other classmates played on a second board game using blue cards that featured two-digit subtraction problems with regrouping. Finally, Jim and one other classmate played on a third game board using yellow cards that featured three-digit subtraction problems with regrouping.

After center time, Ms. Wilson reviewed the student work from each center to assess student progress. This assessment allowed Ms. Wilson to provide feedback to students and plan for the next steps in their learning.

In this example, you can see how Ms. Wilson applied learning centers in a manner that reflected a variety of learning styles. While centers 1 and 3 emphasized more analytical and procedural activities, centers 2 and 4 involved more physical activity (e.g., "macaroni math" and game boards). Although each center had a specific focus, activities within each center were developmentally appropriate for each student. For example, in the problem-solving center, Dorothy worked on one-step addition word problems with single-digit numbers while Jim worked on multi-step subtraction word problems with three-digit numbers and regrouping.

Graphic Organizers

The concept of "a picture is worth a thousand words" comes to life in the flexible and multidimensional strategy of graphic organizers. Gunter, Estes, and Mintz (2007) define graphic organizers as "visual and spatial displays that arrange information graphically so that key concepts and the relation-ships among the concepts are displayed" (p. 287). Depending on the learning strengths or challenges of students, graphic organizers can present information in the linguistic form of print, the nonlinguistic form of pictures or symbols, or a combination of print and symbols. Graphic organizers also can be presented to students in blank form. Students can use the forms to organize and construct specific assignments, or they can gather and organize new information on their own and in cooperative learning groups. In any of these modes, graphic organizers provide students with a strategy to clarify their thinking and process, organize, and prioritize information (Smith & Smith, 2006).

Brain research suggests that forming mental images is very helpful for students as they work on cognitive tasks (Hyerle, 2000). Our personal memories are linked and affected by images. With every image we create, each mental picture is unique. When students create and use mental images to form inter-pretations, clarify their thinking, and assist in understanding, they are deepening their understanding and creating new knowledge.

Figure 1.7 shows an example of an advance graphic organizer that includes information from this chapter that you can use before reading this section to broadly organize your thoughts and ideas. A partially completed organizer is another option that could be presented to students during the learning process. A blank organizer can be given to students after reading or following instruction to help them recall information. Finally, completed organizers can be used later in the learning process for review and reflection (Bursuck & Damer, 2007).

FIGURE 1.7
Sample Advance Graphic Organizer

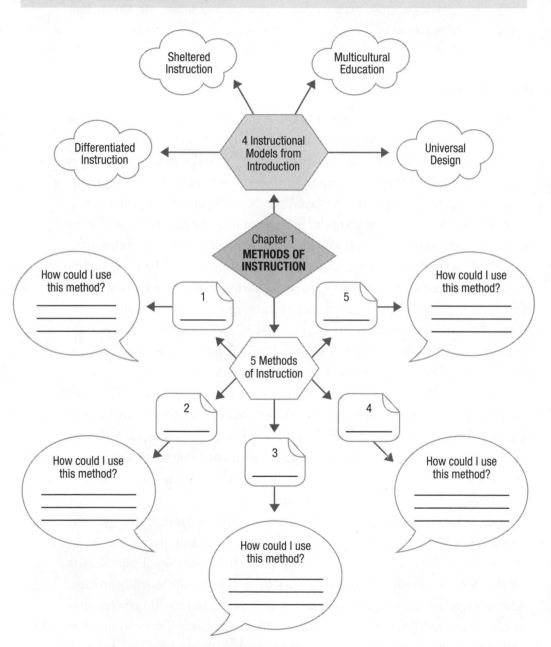

Graphic organizers can be made in an endless number of configurations such as mapping, mind maps, clusters, and webbing. Some of the most commonly used graphic organizer configurations include Know-Want-to-Know-Learned (KWL) charts, Venn diagrams, and story maps. David Hyerle's Thinking Maps (2000) are used effectively in many schools and are effective learning contexts for students. Some examples of thinking maps include the circle thinking map, the bridge map, the bubble map, the double-bubble map, and the cause and effect map. Due to the fact that there are a myriad of graphic organizers, it is helpful to think of graphic organizers as an overriding concept with many configuration options.

Graphic organizers can be constructed in many sizes or shapes. These organizers can be used in a preprinted format, configured in a small format for personal desktop use, displayed on a classroom wall, constructed with paper, connected by yarn to represent different lines, or used with actual objects to complete the configurations.

Technology offers many options for creating graphic organizers. Inspiration is a software program that helps you design graphic organizers with the click of a mouse. The program comes with an extensive image file and you can import your own images. The graphic organizers from Inspiration can be printed in many sizes or projected on a screen or wall using a computer. This program also allows you to add links within the graphic organizer to Web sites, audio files, and podcasts. In addition, Inspiration will compile the information into a traditional outline format without graphics. These organizers can be used with screen readers for students with literacy and reading challenges. It also provides a conversion program that allows you to translate your organizers into different languages.

Applying Graphic Organizers in the Classroom

In Mr. Jones's classroom, he can use graphic organizers with his students in a variety of different ways. For example, he could differentiate his instruction by utilizing a partially completed graphic organizer for one activity and providing instructional materials at different reading levels for his students. Shalandra would benefit from using more complex materials while Juan would gain value from graphic organizers that are embedded into the precepts of multicultural education. Juan could articulate and record what he knows and wants to learn about a topic over time. This information could be posted in the classroom on a wall-sized organizer and used for review (Okolo, Ferretti, & MacArthur, 2005).

Getting the Most Out of Graphic Organizers

Archer and Gleason (1997) suggest the following guidelines for constructing graphic organizers in your classroom:

- **Identify the content to be taught with the graphic organizer.** Once the content is identified, the graphic organizer can be used to help students focus on the salient elements of the content and graphically show how these elements are related.
- **Select the graphic organizer that best fits the content.** For example, if you are teaching students about a specific process, a flow chart may be the best way to present this information.
- **Fill in the graphic organizer prior to using it in instruction.** This helps to ensure that the information you plan to present is clear and accurate.
- **Create a blank map to be used with your students for instruction.** This will allow you to model how to use the graphic organizer.

As you use graphic organizers with your students, Archer and Gleason (1997) suggest the following guidelines:

- **First, students should be taught what type of content is typically displayed in a specific graphic organizer.** For example, the first time a flow chart is used, you can present a blank flow chart, show students how to write the steps of a process in the blank squares of the diagram, and explain that the arrows in between the squares show the order in which the steps occur. You can also explain that flow charts are typically used to show the sequence of events in a process.
- **Although graphic organizers are appropriate for all grade levels, simple formats such as Venn diagrams should be used with primary**

students. Likewise, for younger learners, it may be best to use a limited number of graphic organizers. As learners mature, you can add different types and more complex graphic organizers.

- **Graphic organizers can be used before, during, or after instruction.** Prior to instruction, teachers can give their students a completed graphic organizer to help them establish a mental framework for new content. During a class discussion, a graphic organizer can help students outline the discussion, capture important concepts, and show the relationships between concepts. Individual students or groups of students can use a partially completed graphic organizer to review important concepts and illustrate how these concepts are connected.

- **After students have experience using graphic organizers, they can create graphic organizers on their own to display concepts or vocabulary discussed in class.**

• • •

Although teaching standards in inclusive classrooms with diverse learners is a complex task, there are instructional methods that can be used effectively to reach this goal. Multiple intelligences, cooperative learning, tiered lessons, learning centers, and graphic organizers are powerful instructional methods that integrate differentiated instruction, universal design, sheltered instruction, and multicultural education and allow teachers to simultaneously address the needs of a wide variety of learners. There is no need to have a separate set of methods for each type of learner in your classroom. Successful implementation of standards-based reform in diverse and inclusive classrooms depends upon your ability to integrate the instructional methods that will help you reach a broad spectrum of learners.

Chapter 2 will extend this discussion and focus on the materials of instruction. The instructional materials that can be used to provide greater access to content and greater engagement in learning for diverse students will be explored in more depth.

Resources for Multiple Intelligences

BOOKS

Armstrong, T. (2009). *Multiple intelligences in the classroom.* Alexandria, VA: ASCD.

Bellanca, J. (2008). *200+ active learning strategies and projects for engaging students' multiple intelligences.* Thousand Oaks, CA: Corwin Press.

Campbell, B. (2007). *Handbook of differentiated instruction using the multiple intelligences: Lesson plans and more.* Boston: Allyn and Bacon.

Gardner, H. (2006). *Multiple intelligences: New horizons in theory and practice.* New York: Basic Books.

JOURNAL ARTICLE

Moran, S., Kornhaber, M., & Gardner, H. (2006). Orchestrating multiple intelligences. *Educational Leadership, 64*(1), 22–27.

WEB SITES

Internet 4 Classrooms: http://www.internet4classrooms.com/classroom_organization.htm

Multiple Intelligences: http://lth3.k12.il.us/rhampton/mi/mi.html

Concept to Classroom: http://www.thirteen.org/edonline/concept2class/. This site provides implementation ideas, lesson plans, and video clips.

Resources for Cooperative Learning

BOOKS

Gillies, R. M. (2007). *Cooperative learning: Integrating theory and practice.* Los Angeles: Sage.

Jacobs, G. M., Powers, M. P., & Lol, W. I. (2002). *Teacher's sourcebook for cooperative learning: Practical techniques, basic principles, and frequently asked questions.* Thousand Oaks, CA: Corwin.

Jolliffe, W. (2007). *Cooperative learning in the classroom: Putting it into practice.* Los Angeles: Sage.

JOURNAL ARTICLE

Schniedewind, N., & Davidson, E. (2000). Differentiating cooperative learning. *Educational Leadership, 58*(1), 24–27.

VIDEO

ASCD. (2005). Getting results from cooperative learning video series [Video]. Alexandria, VA: Author.

Resources for Tiered Lessons

BOOK

Adams, C. M., & Pierce, R. L. (2006). *A practical guide to tiered lessons in the elementary grades.* Waco, TX: Prufrock Press.

JOURNAL ARTICLES

Levy, H. M. (2008). Meeting the needs of all students through differentiated instruction: Helping every child meet and exceed standards. *The Clearing House, 81,* 16–166.

Pierce, R. L., & Adams, C. M. (2004). Tiered lessons: One way to differentiate mathematics instruction. *Gifted Child Today, 27*(2), 58–65.

VIDEO

ASCD. (2003). Instructional strategies for the differentiated classroom: Tiered assignments [Video]. Alexandria, VA: Author.

WEB SITES

MBUSD Tiered Lesson Plans: http://www.manhattan.k12.ca.us/staff/pware/diff/. This site provides sample tiered lessons at the elementary, middle, and high school levels in multiple subject areas.

Tiered Curriculum Project: http://www.doe.in.gov/exceptional/gt/tiered_curriculum/welcome.html. This site provides sample tiered lessons at the elementary, middle, and high school levels in multiple subject areas.

Resources for Learning Centers

BOOK

Rice, D. H. (2004). *How to manage learning centers in the classroom.* Westminster, CA: Teacher Created Resources.

JOURNAL ARTICLES

Jarrett, O. (2010). "Inventive" learning stations. *Science and Children, 47*(5), 56–59.

King-Sears, M. E. (2007). Designing and delivering learning center instruction. *Intervention in School and Clinic, 42,* 137–147.

Stephens, H., & Jairells, V. (2003). Weekend study buddies: Using portable learning centers. *Teaching Exceptional Children, 35*(3), 36–39.

VIDEO

ASCD. (2004). Instructional strategies for the differentiated classroom: Centers [Video]. Alexandria, VA: Author.

WEB SITE

Internet for Classrooms: http://www.internet4classrooms.com/classroom_organization.htm. This site includes tips for center use and provides example centers at the elementary, middle, and high school levels.

Resources for Graphic Organizers

BOOKS

Burke, J. (2002). *Tools for thought: Graphic organizers for your classroom.* Portsmouth, NH: Heinemann.

Drapeau, P. (2009). *Differentiating with graphic organizers.* Thousand Oaks, CA: Corwin.

JOURNAL ARTICLES

Baxendell, B. W. (2003). Consistent, coherent, creative: The three C's of graphic organizers. *Teaching Exceptional Children, 35*(3), 46–53.

Gallavan, N. P., & Kottler, E. (2007). Eight types of graphic organizers for empowering social studies students and teachers. *The Social Studies, 98*(3), 117–123.

Gill, S. R. (2007). Learning about word parts with Kidspiration. *The Reading Teacher, 61*(1), 79–84.

Struble, J. (2007). Using graphic organizers as formative assessment. *Science Scope, 30*(5), 69–71.

VIDEO

ASCD. (1999). How to use graphic organizers to promote student thinking [Video]. Alexandria, VA: Author.

WEB SITES

Teacher Tap: http://www.graphicorganizers.com/downloads.htm. This site provides many types of downloadable graphic organizers.

Education Oasis: http://www.educationoasis.com/curriculum/graphic_organizers.htm. This site provides many types of downloadable graphic organizers.

CAST: http://www.cast.org/publications/ncac/ncac_go.html. This site provides information about different types of graphic organizers.

Graphic.Org: http://www.graphic.org/index.html. This site provides downloadable graphic organizers and links to other sites.

2

Supporting the Classroom
with Materials for Instruction

When we consider standards-based reform, we expect that our students will converge and have similar learning outcomes; however, it is not that simple. We need to account for inclusion, which naturally brings a divergence of student learning styles and challenges. As stated in the Introduction, teachers are being called upon to produce greater similarity in learning outcomes, despite greater diversity in student populations. In this chapter, we will address the second element of the MMECCA framework, the **MATERIALS** of instruction, or the tangible items, that are used to support instruction and create outcomes for our diverse students.

Incorporating Universal Design for Learning Principles into the Classroom Design

Materials in the typical general education classroom tend to be limited in scope. Commonly found supplies such as textbooks may be supplemented with student workbooks or worksheets. Sometimes manipulatives and specific multimedia such as number-line sets for math, a globe for social studies, or videos, software, and Internet resources may be used to support learning.

These tools typically function as add-ons to the curriculum rather than as an embedded tool for delivering the curriculum. Many schools and districts do not have the funds to purchase these add-on materials. Students in those districts have few options that can be matched to their learning styles or diverse needs. Alternative formats of basic materials can also be provided for students with disabilities, such as Braille texts for students who are blind, large print text for students with low vision, and CDs with audio output for students with dyslexia (Rose, Meyer, & Hitchcock, 2006).

Materials in a Universal Design for Learning (UDL) classroom are different. These materials will be used to give students multiple means of representation of concepts, multiple means of engaging in learning the concepts, and multiple means of expression for students to demonstrate what they have learned. In a UDL classroom, instruction is more flexible and provides accessibility for all students. Teachers who use the principles of UDL in their classroom recognize that instruction does not come as a one-size-fits-all design. For example, digital content can be presented in different ways to meet the learning needs of each student. This content can include adding hyperlinks and glossaries. It might also include graphs, animation, and videos linked within the body of materials to aid understanding and expand content experience to demonstrate a concept (Rose, Meyer, & Hitchcock, 2006). The UDL principles help teachers create classrooms where students can use technologies to move beyond being academic observers. These principles provide a model for self-actuated learning and universal access for all students. Regardless of students' disabilities or differentiated learning styles, every student needs and has the right to access the curriculum (Nelson, 2006). UDL should be part of the initial design of the curriculum, learning environments, and assessments. Pisha and Coyne (2001) call this approach "smart from the start." The following list includes several Web sites that will further your understanding of UDL.

- **Center for Applied Special Technology (CAST):** http://www.cast.org
- **CAST UDL Lesson Planner:** http://lessonbuilder.cast.org/
- **Digital Content in the Classroom:** http://www.cast.org/teachingevery student/toolkits/tk_introduction.cfm?tk_id=41

- **DO IT:** http://www.washington.edu/doit
- **Planning for All Learners:** http://www.cast.org/teachingeverystudent/ toolkits/tk_introduction.cfm?tk_id=21

In the Introduction, we discussed some of the founding principles of UDL. It is interesting that this term originated in the field of architecture. The tenets for UDL were created to ensure universal access for individuals of all capabilities. Over time, it became obvious that the designs that were originally intended for individuals with disabilities were helpful to everyone. For example, push bars or lever handles for doors replaced traditional doorknobs. This universal design has become helpful to people without disabilities when they carry large parcels, heavy briefcases, or use cell phones. You can learn more about these tenets at the Center for Universal Design's Web site at http://design.ncsu.edu/cud. When we use UDL principles to build the curriculum and select materials for the classroom, all students will have equal opportunities to learn.

Classroom materials should be designed to follow the basic tenets of UDL—providing students with multiple means of representation, engagement, and expression. It is equally important to select materials that help students retain the information. Learning is not useful if students forget what they have learned. According to Rief (1993), students retain

- 10 percent of what they read
- 20 percent of what they hear
- 30 percent of what they see
- 50 percent of what they see and hear
- 70 percent of what they say
- 90 percent of what they say and do

These statistics remind us that it is important to use multisensory material whenever possible. It may not be feasible to use multisensory material for every lesson you teach. As you vary how you present information in your classroom, students will be more engaged in the learning process. Improved student engagement will result in improved achievement. Figure 2.1 shows examples of multiple ways to engage students in diverse classrooms.

FIGURE 2.1

Multiple Ways to Engage Students in Diverse Classrooms

Auditory	Visual	Tactile-Kinesthetic	Affective	Technology Options
Listening to text read aloud	Using a dictionary	Using a Braille dictionary	Working in areas of student interest	Using a talking dictionary
Listening to and retelling directions	Highlighting key points	Touching words on a word wall	Working with a partner who can help with definitions	Downloading and listening to a podcast on an iPod
Asking and answering questions	Outlining steps to solving a problem	Using manipulatives	Working alone or in cooperative groups	Using a word processing program
Engaging in a debate	Completing a graphic organizer	Building a model	Participating in a discussion group or book club	Using a talking calculator
Engaging in a discussion	Designing a poster	Using response cards	Participating in a seminar	Creating spreadsheets
Giving verbal prompts	Illustrating or taking pictures	Using a game format	Giving feedback	Creating a video
Talking through steps	Drawing	Finger spelling	Giving praise	Using blogging or text messaging

From Garguiulo/Metcalf. *Teaching in Today's Inclusive Classrooms*, 1E. © 2010 Wadsworth, a part of Cengage Learning, Inc. Reproduced by permission. www.cengage.com/permissions.

Using Print Resources

Reading instruction in the early elementary grades is focused on learning to read. As children graduate into upper elementary and middle school, the focus shifts to reading to learn. Diamond and Moore (1995) discuss the importance of organizing classrooms to foster partnerships and collaboration among diverse students as they talk, listen, read, think, and write. These collaborations include providing students with experiences that allow them to read to learn. In the next section, we will discuss several important areas to be considered with respect to print resources—visual enhancement, cultural plurality, dictionaries, and other aids.

Using Visual Enhancement

Visually enhanced reading materials can contribute to students' learning experiences. Illustrations with vivid colors and details allow students' imaginations to travel to other times and places (Diamond & Moore, 1995). Exploring the visual details of an environment helps students with reading or language challenges have a better understanding of the context of the reading material. Illustrations also can provide cultural information, open up meaningful literature experiences, and promote dynamic exchanges among diverse students as each person shares his or her interpretation of the story. Visually enhanced reading materials assist struggling readers by

- Providing indicators in the story line to help them anticipate and predict the content of the text.
- Improving their comprehension with visual information that can be more accurately interpreted than language-based information.
- Supporting their ability to recall and retell the story. Many students remember illustrated information for greater lengths of time than text-based information.

Graphic novels are another print resource to use with struggling readers. These novels are similar to comic books, but they have longer and more complex stories. Graphic novels provide the same benefits as illustrated books and are available in electronic formats.

Using Cultural Plurality

Ensuring that print materials reflect a spirit of cultural plurality is important to supporting learning in diverse classrooms. The Council on Interracial Books for Children (1978) offers the following guidelines for evaluating children's books for cultural plurality:

- **Check the illustrations.** Look to see if the illustrations depict a broad range of human diversity, such as race, ethnicity, and gender. Look for stereotypical depictions. Which characters are doing what in the illustrations? Are females and people of color consistently depicted in subservient or passive roles?

- **Check the story line.** Are persons of color or individuals with disabilities required to have superhuman qualities to gain acceptance or approval? Are these characters framed as "the problem"? Are these characters able to solve their own problems or must a white, male, or nondisabled individual come to the rescue? Is the status of the female characters based on their own initiative and intelligence? Or are they dependent upon their good looks or to their relationship to male characters in the story?
- **Consider the author's perspective.** No author can be totally objective. Has the author created a balanced story? Does the author's perspective seem overly patriarchal or feminist? Is the story solely from a Eurocentric perspective? Are diverse cultural perspectives included?

When we are aware of these elements, we can provide reading materials to our students that reflect the ideals of culturally responsive instruction. The resources list at the end of this chapter includes sources that can help you select appropriate reading materials.

Using Dictionaries and Other Aids

Electronic dictionaries are a great multimedia support for children with writing challenges. They come in multiple formats, and students can experiment with different versions until they find one that fits their needs. Electronic dictionaries are easier for most students to use than the traditional print version. For diverse students, electronic dictionaries provide helpful features such as auditory assistance for pronunciation or verifying words that students are seeking.

Electronic dictionaries come in formats that are appropriate for young children and mature learners. Many talking dictionaries for young children are illustrated and give them additional learning support. The following list includes online dictionaries that you can explore:

- **Enchanted Learning Picture Dictionary:** http://www.enchanted learning.com/Dictionary.html
- **Franklin Spelling Ace:** http://www.franklin.com/handhelds/dictionaries/ spell_correctors/

- **Internet Picture Dictionary:** www.pdictionary.com
- **Merriam Webster Online:** http://www.m-w.com

Embedding Content-Rich Experiences into the Classroom

Virtual field trips and tours are great opportunities for students to have content-rich experiences. Teachers can choose a variety of global and national entities to explore, such as NASA, Colonial Williamsburg, the Smithsonian museums, and the Smithsonian National Zoological Park. Some sites offer video streaming observation experiences. For example, the Smithsonian National Zoological Park provides the Pandacam that shows live streaming video of the panda habitat from your choice of two camera views. NASA offers numerous virtual field trips into outer space and across the surface of the earth. Students can follow the daily adventures of scientists and explorers into the far reaches of the earth, watch videos taken from various sites, and e-mail their questions. The Smithsonian museums offer virtual "walking" tours where students can choose what they want to see and walk through as though they are using a video camera. You can explore these virtual tours by using the following links:

- **Colonial Williamsburg:** www.colonialwilliamsburg.com/visit/tourThe Town/NASA:http://search.nasa.gov/search/search.jsp?nasaInclude=virtual+field+trips
- **Pandacam at the Smithsonian National Zoological Park:** http:// national zoo.si.edu/Animals/GiantPandas/default.cfm?cam=LP2
- **Smithsonian Museums:** www.mnh.si.edu/panoramas/#

Skype and iChat are software applications that allow you to explore virtual opportunities such as bringing guest speakers to classes. These programs open up endless opportunities for students to communicate with experts or children from many countries and cultures. You can link to these services from anywhere in the world. For example, by using virtual docent programs, you can pre-arrange a meeting and connect to wonderful tours, lectures, and question-and-answer sessions. These content-rich experiences give students engaging and valuable opportunities for learning. Let's take a look at how Mr. Hogan uses content-rich experiences in his classroom.

Mr. Hogan is a 5th grade teacher at a school in a low socioeconomic neighborhood. Eighty five percent of the students in the school qualify for free or reduced-priced lunches. Ninety percent of his students are minorities and three students are ELLs. Mr. Hogan is certified in elementary and special education and 45 percent of his students have disabilities, the maximum allowed within education laws and mandates. Mr. Hogan is proud of his students. They have worked well in collaborative learning groups throughout the year with great success.

At the end of the year, Mr. Hogan and his class are completing a unit on ecology in jungle environments, and he decides to schedule a trip for his students to visit the local museum of natural history and meet with the educational team and docent. He is aware that most of his students have never visited the museum due to financial and transportation barriers. Mr. Hogan believes that this trip will be beneficial to his students' life experiences. Unfortunately, the trip was denied due to the school's limited funding.

Mr. Hogan decides to explore the possibility of a virtual field trip. He has heard other teachers talking about these types of trips, and he wonders how it will work in his very diverse classroom. When he contacts the museum, they inform him that they would be glad to help with this project. They tell him that the museum has a Web site with a virtual tour as well as a listing of museums around the country that have virtual habitat exhibits. Mr. Hogan is delighted and proceeds with planning.

The class is divided into five collaborative learning teams for this project. Each collaborative group is a heterogeneous mix of students that is representative of Mr. Hogan's class. Each student is assigned a lead role within his or her group. Each group will make a 10-minute presentation about life in a jungle habitat that includes related study and support materials to be shared with the class. Each group has a film director, a recorder, a wiki director, a spokesperson, and a trip coordinator. Based on each member's strengths and challenges, the following roles are developed, negotiated, and agreed upon:

- The **film director** is responsible for capturing images for the group presentation. Videos can be downloaded from YouTube, TeacherTube, Google and still images can be downloaded from a museum's or zoo's Web site. The director will load these videos and images to the wiki for review. After all group members give feedback on their preferences, the film director edits the media resources on the wiki. This role would be a good choice for a child with disabilities because these students typically thrive in a technological environment.

- The **recorder** is in charge of recording the dialogue that will be used to narrate the presentation and compiling all contributed material. The recorder will create a wiki page that lists all the contributions that are expected from all group members. This role is a great role for a student with strong writing skills.

- The **wiki director** will develop the group's Web presence. This responsibility includes creating an engaging appearance and working closely with the recorder to include accurate information. The recorder will provide most of the written work to support the wiki director. This would be another good role for a child with a disability.

- The **spokesperson** will be the primary presenter for the group. This role includes making arrangements with Mr. Hogan for the group's interaction with the museum personnel, gathering questions from each group member, recording and archiving audio files of the conferences and the group's presentation, and posting files to the wiki in collaboration with the wiki director.

- The **trip coordinator** works closely with Mr. Hogan to ensure that the group is tuned in when they need to be. This person is responsible for posting directions on the wiki for all needed resources. The trip coordinator will also coordinate with the ESL teacher to make sure that all information is presented in other languages as necessary. This role will require organizational skills and can be filled by an ELL student.

With technology, there is a place and role for everyone!

Creating Motion-Centered Experiences in the Classroom

Meaningful manipulatives are multisensory tools that are very beneficial for students with diverse learning styles. Earlier in this chapter, we talked about globes and number lines as examples of manipulatives. Working with manipulatives can be more like an integrative brain function when used in motion-centered experiences. TouchMath is a good example of one such set of tools. For this multisensory math program, students begin by using concrete materials such as beans or pieces of cereal to practice counting. Students soon move on to touching points on the manipulated numeral set and other materials that come with the program. Over time, students are able to learn the content by simply using other surfaces for tapping out numbers or using visualizations of previous problem-solving techniques to help them remember math concepts and calculations. For more information, you can log onto www.touchmath.com for free downloads and videos.

Using Auditory Materials in the Classroom

Auditory materials come in an increasing number of formats and can be classified in multiple ways. MP3 players are very popular, pocket-sized devices that play music and other types of audio recordings. Students can use them to play podcasts such as archived recordings from their classes or information transferred from other sites. MP3 players provide flexible access and give students the ability to repeat recordings for clarification and additional information. Many electronic books are available as free downloads in MP3 formats for pleasure or extended learning opportunities.

Amazon offers the Kindle 2, which delivers text-to-speech playback for an extensive list of books, newspapers, and blogs. You can also use this device for your own documents. This device opens up many additional avenues of access for students with reading challenges. The National Instructional Materials Accessibility Standard (NIMAS) requires textbook publishers to produce standard source files that allow their publications to be easily translated into talking books, Braille, and large-print formats. For students who have challenges reading print, alternative formats help them with their reading difficulties.

NIMAS was established as part of the reauthorization of Individuals with Disabilities Education Act (IDEA) in 2004. NIMAS provisions apply to students with identified print disabilities who have an Individualized Education Program (IEP). Check out the NIMAS site (http://nimas.cast.org) for more information and program updates. Bookshare is a partner with NIMAS and the U.S. Department of Education and offers many audio book options. You can visit Bookshare at www.bookshare.org.

Infusing Popular Culture into Instruction

Today's students have increased exposure to multimedia and pop culture technology resources. Some teachers may question whether there is any value in using these specific resources and other computer- and Internet-based activities. According to the U.S. Department of Education Office of Educational Technology (2004), students' computer skills are far beyond those of their teachers. These students, often referred to as the Millennials, prefer to use the Internet and seek information that is more abundant, accessible, and up-to-date. In a 2004 report, the U.S. Department of Education cited the following facts for today's students:

- 49 percent of students may be interested in pursuing careers in technology.
- 28 percent of high school students access foreign news services via the Internet.
- 94 percent of teens use the Internet for school-related research.
- Students spend more time on the Internet than they do watching television.
- The largest group of new users of the Internet from 2000–02 were 2- to 5-year-olds.
- Today's students feel technology is an essential and preferred asset in every part of their lives.
- Today's students are ultra communicators.
- Computers can help students increase their performance on standardized tests.

- Technology can increase students' motivation and improve their self-concept.
- Technology promotes inclusion for students with disabilities. (p. 11)

For educators, it is essential to blend these facts into the teaching and learning process.

Using Web 2.0 Tools

What is Web 2.0? This term generally refers to a group of new Internet applications that promote the use of, contribution to, and creation of information. Blogs, wikis, podcasting, and social networking are some of the most widely used applications (Churchill, 2007).

- **Blogs**—Students can use blogs for discussions with friends or other groups of individuals. They can be integrated as digital bulletin boards where students can share, self-evaluate, and participate in group evaluations and feedback sessions. Students can also include art and photography on their blogs. Blogs also hold great promise for use in journaling in student activities (Utecht, 2007).
- **Wikis**—Wikis are Internet-based collections of information that can be as expansive as Wikipedia or as simple as compiling information into a camping trip organizer. Teachers can use wikis for adding information to research topics, posting outstanding student work, or reporting news to parents on a bulletin board. You can visit Wikispaces at www.wikispaces.com to build a wiki to support your classes.
- **Podcasting**—Podcasts are easy and affordable audio recordings of activities or presentations that students can listen to on their personal MP3 players. Students can use podcasts to access new information, record their own presentations, and review content that is presented or archived in this format.
- **Social Networking**—Social networking sites such as MySpace and Facebook provide great opportunities for students to link and communicate with students from all over the world. For diverse students, these

sites can promote and improve their writing abilities. As always, teachers need to monitor students' participation for Internet safety issues.

The following links are great resources that provide more in-depth information on Web 2.0 applications:

- **Blogs in Plain English:** http://www.youtube.com/watch?v=NN2I 1pWXjXI
- **Podcasting in Plain English:** http://www.youtube.com/watch?v=y-MSL 42NV3c
- **Social Media in Plain English:** http://www.youtube.com/watch?v=Mp IOClX1jPE&feature=channel
- **Twitter in Plain English:** http://www.youtube.com/watch?v=ddO9id max0o
- **Wikis in Plain English:** http://www.youtube.com/watch?v=-dnL00TdmLY
- **TeacherTube:** http://www.teachertube.com
- **You Tube:** http://www.youtube.com

• • •

Instructional materials are critical for successful teaching in any classroom, especially in diverse and inclusive classrooms where students' skill levels, learning styles, and interests are more varied. There are many exciting options that can help teachers meet the instructional challenges they face.

In Chapter 3, we will explore other factors related to the context of instruction in diverse and inclusive classrooms.

Resources for Multicultural Materials

BOOKS

Bar, C., East, K. A., & Thomas, R. L. (2007). *Across cultures: A guide to multicultural literature for children.* Santa Barbara, CA: Libraries Unlimited.

Knowles, E., & Smith, M. (2007). *Understanding diversity through novels and picture books.* Santa Barbara, CA: Libraries Unlimited.

JOURNAL ARTICLES

Davis, K. L., Brown, B. G., Liedel-Rice, A., & Soeder, P. (2005). Experiencing diversity through children's multicultural literature. *Kappa Delta Pi Record, 41*(4), 176–179.

Levin, F. (2007). Encouraging ethical respect through multicultural literature. *The Reading Teacher, 61*(1), 101–104.

Lowery, R. M., & Sabis-Burns, D. (2007). From borders to bridges: Making cross-cultural connections through multicultural literature. *Multicultural Education, 14*(4), 50–54.

WEB SITES

Teaching Tolerance: www.teachingtolerance.org. This site is a project of the Southern Poverty Law Center. It includes a wealth of information related to culturally responsive instruction. Teachers can request free instructional kits related to topics such as the civil rights movement and the holocaust. This site also includes reviews of multicultural children's literature.

Cooperative Children's Book Center: http://www.education.wisc.edu/ccbc/books/multi cultural.asp. This site includes annotated bibliographies of high-quality multicultural children's literature for grades K-12.

Multicultural Children's Literature: http://www.multiculturalchildrenslit.com. This site includes annotated bibliographies of high-quality multicultural children's literature for grades K-12.

Resources for Technology

BOOKS

Dell, A. G., Newton, D. A., & Petroff, J. G. (2008). *Assistive technology in the classroom: Enhancing the school experiences of students with disabilities.* Upper Saddle River, NJ: Merrill.

Shelly, G. B., Cashman, T. J., Gunter, R. E., & Gunter, G. A. (2010). *Integrating technology and digital media in the classroom.* Boston: Thomson.

JOURNAL ARTICLES

Bausch, M. E., & Ault, M. J. (2008). Assistive technology implementation plan: A tool for improving outcomes. *Teaching Exceptional Children, 41*(1), 6–14.

Columbo, M. W., & Columbo, P. D. (2007). Blogging to improve instruction in differentiated science classrooms. *Phi Delta Kappan, 89*(1), 60–63.

Davis, A., & McGrail, E. (2009). "Proof-revising" with podcasting: Keeping readers in mind as students listen to and rethink their writing. *The Reading Teacher, 62*(6), 522–529.

Lucking, R. A., Christmann, E. P., & Wighting, M. J. (2009). Podcasts and blogs. *Science Scope, 33*(3), 64–67.

Putnam, S. M., & Kingsley, T. (2009). The atoms family: Using podcasts to enhance the development of science vocabulary. *The Reading Teacher, 63*(2), 100–108.

Simpson, C. G., McBride, R., Spencer, V. G., Lowdermilk, J., & Lynch, S. (2009). Assistive technology: Supporting learners in inclusive classrooms. *Kappa Delta Pi Record, 45*(4), 172–175.

3

Creating an Environment for Instruction

Perhaps one of the greatest challenges teachers encounter is creating the ideal classroom environment that both nurtures and propels students to learn. As educators, we have a clear mandate to thoughtfully consider the type of learning environment that will have the maximum positive effect on the students in our care. Such an environment cannot materialize by attending to only one dimension of the classroom climate. We must consider how we facilitate the academic concerns of teaching and learning as well as shaping the overall physical, emotional, and social aspects of the classroom that will support each learner's overall development and sense of well-being.

When teachers work toward constructing a cooperative and collaborative atmosphere, the potential for students to gain the knowledge, skills, attitudes, and behaviors essential for learning expands. An effective classroom manager is similar to an orchestra conductor. Conductors possess a keen awareness of all the instruments, sounds, and players while simultaneously attending to the quality of the total musical output. Teachers must have a well-developed awareness of each learner's characteristics and needs; craft harmonious and synergistic classroom dynamics; and employ worthwhile rules, procedures, and consequences to ensure that all students have the greatest opportunity to meet standards-based outcomes.

How we carry out these actions can either enhance or sabotage our teaching and learning efforts. In this chapter, we will focus on the third element of the MMECCA framework, the **ENVIRONMENTS** of instruction that will help you promote positive behavior, create physical arrangements for the classroom, and facilitate an inclusive classroom community.

Promoting Positive Behavior

In the absence of a supportive environment, learning cannot occur. Reducing inappropriate behavior is a critical aspect of creating such an environment. Proactive strategies to reduce these behaviors include planning appropriate learning activities, establishing explicit and reasonable behavioral expectations, using positive behavior supports, and considering individual differences. Despite the effectiveness of these strategies, inappropriate behaviors will still occur. This realization underscores our need to have a repertoire of effective strategies to respond to inappropriate behaviors. In the following discussion, we present strategies for reducing and responding to inappropriate behaviors.

Planning Appropriate Learning Activities for Students

One of the most important and proactive things teachers can do to head off inappropriate behavior is to ensure that the learning activities in the classroom are appropriate for students. All activities should reflect the myriad skill and ability levels of the students in the class. If class activities are too difficult or too easy for students, they will find something else to do—and most of the time, it won't be something desirable. Students are more likely to act out when they are frustrated or bored.

Classroom activities should be engaging. As discussed in Chapter 1, it's important to tap into students' strengths and interests. Your own demeanor and level of enthusiasm also influences students' perceptions of classroom activities. If you can create an environment where students are engaged, coercive strategies are not needed.

Establishing Explicit and Reasonable Behavioral Expectations for Students

Intuitiveness and social judgment often are areas of weakness for some students with disabilities. Likewise, students who are unfamiliar with the school's culture will not know the behavior expectations unless they are explicitly told. It is especially important in diverse, inclusive classrooms for teachers to clearly articulate these expectations. The following guidelines are helpful in establishing classroom rules:

- **Use classroom rules that state desired behaviors rather than undesired behaviors.** For example, creating the following rule, "Come to class with all needed supplies" is more effective than "Don't depend on others for your supplies." If a classroom rule or policy is stated negatively, the student does not know what the desired behavior is. Students will have to infer what they are supposed to do. Classroom rules also should be clearly posted.
- **Make sure classroom rules are reasonable.** Classroom rules should only include behaviors that students are capable of performing consistently. For example, a classroom rule that states "Remain in your seats throughout the day" may be unreasonable because students will inevitably have to get up for something.
- **Create a manageable number of classroom rules.** Less is more! Keep the list down to five to eight rules. It is difficult for many students to remember a long list of rules. Ensure that the rules or procedures you select are critical to the classroom learning environment.
- **Clearly state the consequences for violating classroom rules or policies.** These consequences should be reasonable, consistently enforced, and allow for human error. For example, if a student calls out in the classroom, you may want to give him or her one warning before a consequence is levied. If consequences are reasonable and allow for human error, you will find it easier to consistently implement them.
- **Clearly explain classroom rules and consequences at the beginning of the school year or term.** For example, if the classroom rule is "Come to class with all needed supplies," then teachers need to specify what the

needed supplies are. If a student brings books, paper, and pencil to school, but he leaves them in his locker, is this a violation of the rule? Can the student request to go to his locker to get his supplies without penalty? Make time to clarify any misconceptions your students might have.

- **Remember to acknowledge appropriate behaviors when they occur.** Try not to focus all of your attention on students who are behaving inappropriately. Praise those students who are meeting behavioral expectations. Positive reinforcement is particularly important for students who struggle in this area. Keep in mind that while elementary students may welcome public acknowledgments, secondary students may prefer more discreet, individual acknowledgments.

- **Consider allowing students the opportunity to establish behavioral expectations.** By the time most students are in 3rd grade, they can meaningfully participate in the process of establishing the rules and consequences that will guide behaviors in their classroom community. By allowing students to participate in this process, you create greater student ownership in the learning environment and a greater appreciation of why rules exist. This ownership increases the likelihood that students will respect the rules that have been established because they had a hand in shaping them.

Using Positive Behavior Supports

Positive behavior supports are strategies that enhance students' capacity to meet behavioral expectations. Modeling and role-plays are common methods that teachers use to directly teach appropriate behaviors. For example, students need to be able to disagree amicably during activities such as cooperative learning. As you teach this skill, you can discuss its importance, model the behavior for students, and provide appropriate and inappropriate examples of the behavior. Students could then be asked to create role-play activities and act out examples of the behavior.

Teaching social problem-solving skills to students also helps them develop appropriate behaviors. This approach helps students become more reflective decision makers and take more responsibility for their actions. Consequence mapping is a social problem-solving technique where students can graphically map out behavioral options and related consequences for a given incident. In the following scenario, we revisit Mr. Jones's classroom and see how he uses a graphic organizer to frame a scenario for his students.

Mr. Jones notices that some of his students are not taking responsibility for their behavior and the resulting consequences. He often overhears them saying things like, "The teacher gave me an 'F' " or "The teacher put me out," as though they had no role in these consequences. To address this concern, he decides to use consequence mapping.

He says to his students, "Imagine you are sitting in your desk, minding your own business and another student comes along and bumps up against you. What would you do?" One student responds, "I would hit that student back." Mr. Jones accepts this response and records it on the graphic organizer. He recognizes that his role is not to critique the students' choices, but to encourage them to consider the consequences of their choices and make the appropriate decisions. He responds, "That's right. You could **decide** to hit them back," emphasizing the fact that this decision is a choice. "But," he continues "if you decided to do that, what might happen afterwards? What might be the consequence?" Another student responds, "You could get in trouble." Mr. Jones acknowledges this response and writes it on the organizer. He continues the discussion and asks, "What else might happen?" A student says, "You could get beat up." Mr. Jones records this response and asks students if they like these consequences. They respond "No." Then he says, "These are the things that could happen if you made **the choice** to hit someone. If you don't like these things, you need to make a different choice. Is there anything else you could decide to do?" The students then give other behavioral options such as tell the teacher, ignore the student who bumped them, and ask the student why he bumped them. Mr. Jones explores the consequences associated with each of these choices and emphasizes to students that when they decide to behave in a certain way, certain consequences are likely to follow. He notes that it is their responsibility to consider all their options, make the best choice, and be prepared for the consequences. Mr. Jones reminds them that no one can "make them get into trouble."

Bibliotherapy is another way that you can teach and reinforce appropriate behaviors to your students. You can select books that feature characters who are struggling with behavioral issues similar to the student. For example, if a student is dealing with anger management, he or she can read and discuss books such as *The Very Angry Day That Amy Didn't Have* by Lawrence Shapiro (1994). After the student reads the book, you and the student can talk about and explore the successful and unsuccessful actions of the lead characters.

Considering Cultural and Learning Differences in the Classroom

Considering cultural and learning differences is important to every aspect of diverse, inclusive classrooms. Many of these differences have important implications for promoting positive behavior. In the next section, we discuss these differences and their implications for behavior management.

Responding to Students with Disabilities

Students with behavioral disorders often experience behavioral challenges that significantly interfere with their learning. These students may exhibit externalizing behaviors such as physical or verbal aggressiveness or internalizing behaviors such as being excessively withdrawn. They may also be oppositional or noncompliant, have compulsive behaviors, or experience mood disorders such as depression. Students with autism also have characteristics that have implications for behavior management. These students often have difficulty establishing and maintaining relationships with others and expressing their wants and needs. Students with autism may also respond in an aggressive manner when frustrated or frightened. They often need a high degree of structure and consistency. Other disability areas, such as learning disabilities, attention-deficit-hyperactivity-disorder (ADHD), and mild mental retardation have been associated with hyperactivity, impulsivity, immature behaviors, and poor social problem-solving skills.

Given these characteristics, as educators in inclusive settings we must be prepared to augment our overall behavior management plans. For some students, it's important to identify and avoid things that tend to trigger inappropriate behaviors. If you are a teacher of a student with autism, you should strive to maintain as much consistency in this student's schedule as possible. When schedule changes are unavoidable, alert and prepare this student for these changes ahead of time.

For some students, it may be necessary to create individualized plans for behavior management that augment the overall classroom plan. For example, a behavior progress monitoring form, such as the one shown in Figure 3.1,

FIGURE 3.1
Behavior Progress Monitoring Form

Name_____ Date_____

Please label each section with "Y" for Yes and "N" for No.

	Period 1	Period 2	Period 3	Period 4	Period 5	Period 6
Brought supplies						
Worked productively						
Was respectful of others						
Teacher's initials						

Period 1 Comments _____

_____

Period 2 Comments _____

_____

Period 3 Comments _____

_____

Period 4 Comments _____

_____

Period 5 Comments _____

_____

Period 6 Comments _____

_____

Parent Signature _____

might be useful with students who need more frequent and structured behavioral monitoring and reinforcement. Using monitoring forms allows you to give behavioral feedback and reinforcement to students at regular intervals throughout the day. These tools will also help you identify behavior patterns in your students.

A behavioral contract is another strategy that you can use to supplement the overall classroom management plan. If a student constantly calls out in class, you can create a contractual agreement with the student to help him or her reduce this behavior.

Responding to Culturally Diverse Students

Within diverse classrooms, the probability of misunderstandings and misrepresentations between teachers and students increases. Some behaviors that we take for granted and accept as normal may be quite different for our students. It is important for us to consider how culturally influenced factors can affect students' classroom behavior.

Interaction styles can vary by culture. For example, in some cultures it may not be appropriate for more than one person to speak at a time or for a speaker to use a loud voice to be heard. Likewise, in some cultures, a higher level of physical activity and verbal discourse may go hand in hand with thinking and learning (Grossman, 1995). If you are working with students from cultures that value interdependence, build in opportunities for these students to engage in cooperative learning or other types of physical activity during the day. If you have behavioral expectations related to using quiet voices or one student talking at a time, set aside time to demonstrate, practice, and reinforce these behaviors with students as needed.

Attitudes about sharing and respecting personal space may also vary by culture. For example, some cultures may embrace communal property rights or the idea that "What's mine is yours and what's yours is mine." This mind-set can lead to conflicts between students if there is not a shared understanding about this issue. Likewise, tolerance for entering personal body space is also culturally influenced. In some cultures, speakers are expected to remain at least two feet apart when they speak. Moving any closer could be interpreted as an overture toward intimacy or as a gesture of aggression (Grossman, 1995).

When working with culturally diverse groups of students, it is important to have explicit discussions regarding expectations about personal space and personal property.

Responding to and determining who is an authority figure are other areas influenced by cultural differences. For example, in some cultures, children recognize all adults as figures of authority. In other cultures, adults may be viewed as authority figures only if they hold certain positions, such as teachers or policemen. In still other cultures, being recognized as an authority figure is based on behavior and not automatically given because of status or position (Grossman, 1995). Therefore, you need to be aware that your students may not automatically view you as an authority figure. You may need to earn this status from your students.

The manner in which deference is shown to authority figures also varies by culture. For example, avoiding eye contact with authority figures is a way of showing respect in some cultures. In other cultures, this same behavior could be interpreted as a sign of indifference or an indicator of deceit (Grossman, 1995). Similarly, responses to classroom management styles can be culturally influenced. Some students will respond to more straightforward directives from authority figures rather than to "politeness formulas" and indirect discourse strategies (e.g., "Sally sit down!" versus "Sally, would you like to sit down?") (Weinstein, Curran, & Tomlinson-Clarke, 2003).

Managing Inappropriate Behaviors

Even if we follow all of the previous guidelines to prevent disruptions, they will still occur! When this happens, remember to remain in control of the situation, avoid escalating the behavior, and try to understand the student's behavior. In the next section, we will explore specific strategies related to these techniques.

Remaining in Control

When behavior problems occur, try to avoid appearing unsettled or thrown off your game. Respond calmly to the student by redirecting the behavior. Give students a warning if it is appropriate. If disciplinary action is necessary, administer the consequence in accordance with classroom policies. Kapalka (2009) suggests the following steps for administering disciplinary action:

- **Initiate disciplinary action by using an attentional cue.** You can begin by getting the student's attention by using his or her name. Make sure the student is aware that you are addressing him or her and that the student is listening.
- **Use a command to redirect the student.** Don't yell. Be sure to make an imperative statement rather than a request (e.g., "Tom, please take your seat" rather than "Tom, would you mind taking your seat?")
- **Give only one directive at a time.** Avoid excess verbiage. Don't debate or give a lengthy explanation.
- **Acknowledge the student's compliance with verbal or nonverbal praise.** When the student corrects the behavior, you can recognize it by saying, "Thank you" or "I like the way you responded." You can also nod affirmatively toward the student.

Understanding Students' Inappropriate Behavior

When inappropriate behaviors occur repeatedly with a student, carefully observe the behavior to determine why the behavior is occurring and what function or purpose it serves. You can begin examining the student's behavior by using the Antecedents, Behavior, and Consequences (ABC) model for functional behavior assessment. To conduct an ABC functional behavior assessment, you can start by examining the events or contexts that seem to precipitate the inappropriate behavior. These events or contexts are referred to as the **antecedents** of the behavior. For example, if a student has a tendency to become physically aggressive, are there any identifiable events or contexts that seem to trigger this aggression? Try to identify a pattern of when these incidents occur and in what contexts they seem most frequent.

Next, think about how the **behavior** happens. If you have a physically aggressive student, how does his or her aggression normally occur? Is it generally directed at the same person? Is it a short outburst? Does it take a while to build? Are there outward signs that the behavior is about to happen? What emotions seem most apparent? Anger? Fear? Hurt?

Finally, consider the **consequences** for the student after the inappropriate behavior occurs. Is the student removed from the classroom or learning activity? Is the targeted student reduced to tears? Does the teacher or other adult spend a great deal of time with the student after the incident occurs? Does the student receive lots of peer attention? How does the student respond to the consequence that ensues?

By using the ABC model for functional behavior assessment, you can examine why inappropriate behavior recurs, look at what needs these actions satisfy for the student, and help students substitute more appropriate behaviors. If the student is seeking attention, you can find more appropriate ways to respond to the student. If the student is using an avoidance strategy like purposefully getting thrown out of the classroom to avoid an undesired activity, think about how you can redirect the student's attention by assigning work that is more appropriate to the student's skills and interests. When students use power plays, such as exerting control over others, making another student cry, or knocking the teacher off of his or her game, explore ways that you can help the student feel more empowered in more appropriate ways. It is important to determine **why** the student seems compelled to repeat the behavior so that you can deal with the underlying cause. Simply trying to squelch the behavior through sanctions or disciplinary action is often ineffective.

Responding to inappropriate behavior is no easy task! However, sometimes you can respond to these behaviors by collaborating with other teachers and parents. Regardless of the degree of support you receive, having tools to address difficult situations is essential. One model that may be helpful for any teacher is the Problem-Solving Approach (PSA) developed by Cruickshank, Jenkins, and Metcalf (2009). This approach includes the following stages:

- Stage 1: Identify the problem and its ownership.
- Stage 2: Determine the value of the goal.
- Stage 3: Analyze the problem situation.
- Stage 4: Rate the proposed solutions.
- Stage 5: Implement and evaluate the best solution.

You met Ms. Wilson in Chapter 1. She is an experienced teacher at Southside Elementary School. Her classes have become more culturally and linguistically diverse during her 20 years of teaching at the school. It is the beginning of the year, and Ms. Wilson is noticing that conflicts are arising with her students. She is very concerned about these clashes because she strongly believes in developing a classroom climate that is collegial and cooperative. She understands that given the diversity of her classroom, students must be able to work collaboratively. Ms. Wilson realizes that she must act quickly so that the sentiments that are developing in the classroom do not continue.

First, Ms. Wilson begins to pay close attention to the arguments and determines that there are two basic groups—students who speak English and students who speak Hmong or Spanish. She decides that she needs to identify and analyze when the arguments are occurring. She decides to keep these daily dated observations on Post-It notes. At the end of the day, she transfers these notes into a notebook. As she reviews her notes, she begins to see a pattern. Ms. Wilson notices the nonverbal signals from her native English-speaking students when she asks them to wait while she devotes time to her ELL students. In addition, she sees the body language of the native English-speaking students when she pairs them together with ELL students. She begins to think that perhaps the native English-speaking students resent both the time she spends with the ELLs and the time they are asked to work with them.

Ms. Wilson weighs whether a whole class meeting should be devoted to her observations or if she should approach specific native English-speaking students who seem to be most upset. She decides that she will begin each class sharing with them about how she values the classroom community and shares specific examples of when she sees them. She also becomes more welcoming of native English-speaking students when they have questions. In addition, she employs more flexible grouping patterns and makes sure that students have the opportunity to work with their friends, too. After several days, Ms. Wilson begins to see a decrease in the arguing between the groups, and students appear to be more satisfied with the new arrangement. Ms. Wilson is pleased with the outcome and decides that she will continue to pay close attention to new conflicts that arise.

Designing the Physical Environment

Teachers must be mindful of the classroom's physical environment to ensure that students avoid injuries and maximize their learning. Thoughtful consideration should always be given to the needs of each member of your classroom community. The manner in which materials, equipment, and furniture are arranged can seriously affect a child's self-esteem, security and comfort, autonomy, self-control, and peer interaction (Jalongo & Isenberg, 2004). The following discussion will highlight important factors to consider with respect to seating arrangements and other aspects of the physical environment.

Using Seating Arrangements

Seating arrangements can facilitate or detract from instructional efficiency. In diverse, inclusive classrooms, it is important to consider how seating can be used to support a variety of instructional approaches.

Using Seating Arrangements to Promote Safety, Encourage Cooperative Learning, and Guide Instructional Approaches

Whether you are a kindergarten teacher or a high school teacher, flexible seating designs, such as dyads, triads, quads, and individual seats support diverse instructional strategies and learning styles. Thoughtful and strategic furniture arrangement and seating plans contribute to students' physical safety, support the teacher's instructional delivery choices, and influence the entire classroom ethos.

According to Weinstein and colleagues (2003), "physical setting can promote social interaction and prosocial behavior. Desks arranged in clusters allow students to work together on activities, share materials, have small-group discussions, and help each other with assignments" (p. 3). Cooperative learning groups have the potential to provide opportunities for students who might not necessarily share ideas and information.

In some cases, you may want students to work independently. If you want to support a student's ability to work as an individual, traditional desks in rows may be more effective (Evertson, Emmer, & Worsham, 2006). We recognize that not all students will perform well when seated in group-like patterns. Wheldall and Lam (1987, as cited in Miller, 2009) suggest that some students with disabilities are more productive and exhibit more "on-task behavior" when they are seated in rows. This seating arrangement appears to significantly reduce the rate of disruptive behavior.

In secondary classrooms, flexible grouping patterns encourage collaboration, help students dismantle long-held stereotypes about other cultural groups, and discourage cliques that tend to dominate middle and high school settings. Effective teachers understand that the physical design of the classroom environment can enhance motivation and have a strong effect on student learning and behavior (Miller, 2009).

Seating arrangements in inclusive, standards-based classrooms need to be designed with diverse students' needs in mind. For example, students with sensory impairments, physical disabilities, and learning or behavioral disabilities can be affected by factors such as seating in high-traffic areas or in proximity to visuals. Figure 3.2 outlines special seating considerations for students with disabilities.

Using Seating Arrangements to Incorporate Students' Cultural Preferences and Promote Intercultural Interactions

Cultural diversity should also be considered with respect to seating arrangements. For example, some cultures emphasize cooperation and group achievement. Members of these cultural groups may feel most comfortable and perform best when the class is arranged to promote interaction and collaboration (Lewis & Doorlag, 1996). Likewise, some cultural groups have fluid boundaries in their homes, and many activities occur simultaneously in the same area. For example, the television may be on while students complete their homework or multiple conversations may be occurring while music is playing. Some cultural groups may be more comfortable with multitasking and working together. Therefore, students from these cultures may be more comfortable with seating arrangements that facilitate these behaviors (Miller, 2009; Weinstein, Curran, & Tomlinson-Clarke, 2003).

Seating patterns can also be used to promote intercultural interactions and interactions between students with disabilities and their peers. Students who have the opportunity to interact with others from different backgrounds

FIGURE 3.2
Seating Considerations for Students with Disabilities

Disability	Challenges to Student	Accommodation by Teacher
Hearing Loss	• Depends on lipreading	• Allow the student to sit in the center of room for clear access to see the teacher's mouth • Provide a swivel chair that the student can use and move to follow class discussions • Use a semicircle seating arrangement to allow the student to hear and lipread all of their classmates • Allow the student to sit next to a competent peer who can assist the student during fire drills and intercom messages
Vision Loss	• Has limited vision • Is at risk for tripping or falling • Depends on hearing teacher's voice	• Allow the student to sit in a seat where bright light comes over his shoulder and allows him to use his non-dominant hand to help reduce light glare as needed • Sit the student away from walking paths, doorways, and learning centers in the classroom • Sit the student close to the teacher or near a responsible peer who can help
Physical Disability (mobility)	• Needs a wheelchair, walker, or crutches to maneuver	• Create an aisle or a pathway at least 32 inches wide so that the student can maneuver easily and safely to key places around the classroom • Place the student's desk near a wall outlet if he or she needs additional power for an electrically powered wheelchair • Think about the height and shape (e.g., sharp edges) of the furniture
Learning Disabilities	• Has difficulty with environmental distractions • Has difficulty with social skills	• Position the student's desk away from doorways, windows, and cluttered areas • Place the student's desk in quieter areas of the classroom during independent seatwork activities • Be sure to provide opportunities for the student to interact with his or her peers
Behavioral Difficulties	• Needs frequent reinforcement and monitoring	• Sit the student near the teacher or near students who can model appropriate classroom behavior • Keep some distance between student desks as needed

Adapted from *Validated practices for teaching students with diverse needs and abilities* (2nd ed.) (pp. 116–118) by S. P. Miller, 2009, Upper Saddle River, NJ: Pearson. Adapted with permission.

can gain valuable insight. Seating arrangements can be used to facilitate this goal. Split-half arrangements, such as seating students in two sections or in two-by-two rows and semicircular arrangements, such as U-shape formations, increase teacher-student and student-to-student interactions (Henley, 2006; Ridling, 1994; both cited in Miller, 2009).

Creating a stimulating environment for learning where students of any age or cultural group feel comfortable and safe requires a great deal of thought, knowledge, and planning. Consider how Ms. Williams arranges her classroom in the following scenario.

Ms. Williams is a middle school art teacher with a diverse, inclusive class. Her school is located in the inner city, characterized as hard to staff, and has suffered from high teacher attrition rates and high transiency rates among students. Three-quarters of her students are African American and close to 90 percent of students receive free or reduced-priced lunches. Ms. Williams teaches approximately 150 students daily. Eighteen students have learning disabilities, mild mental retardation, emotional disturbances, speech impairments, or visual impairment. At the beginning of the school year, she is already having difficulty with two of her students, Charles and Jared. Ms. Williams mentions this problem to another teacher who says, "Yes, I know them. They're Special Ed! What can you do?"

Immediately, Ms. Williams rearranges her seating plan. To ensure that Charles and Jared do not feel singled out, she assigns seats to all students. Charles and Jared will be seated at a distance from each other but near enough to Ms. Williams so that they will be able to see her nonverbal signals. Next, Ms. Williams contacts the collaborative teacher in the school. Ms. Williams will confer with the building's collaborative teacher or school district special education supervisor about the students' IEPs and the possible interventions for these students in the event that she or an aide is not available for her class.

Ms. Williams will have individual conferences with Charles and Jared and review what behaviors are acceptable and unacceptable in this class. She will provide logical explanations for why the behaviors are being requested and the subsequent consequences for each infringement. Charles and Jared will have adequate time to ask questions and practice these behaviors. For the remainder of the year, she will focus on reinforcing positive behavior and providing frequent verbal and nonverbal feedback in a timely fashion. If either student misbehaves, her response will be specific and immediate. Though Ms. Williams may be tempted to provide public positive feedback to her students, she knows that secondary students prefer individual feedback. She may experiment with using other reinforcement such as touching a student on the shoulder or giving the student a tangible reward or token that can later be exchanged for previously determined privileges.

Designing Other Aspects of the Physical Environment

In addition to seating arrangements, other aspects of the physical environment, such as classroom bulletin boards and displays, are important factors in shaping students' learning experience.

Students should see themselves reflected in the physical environment. All bulletin boards and classroom displays should reflect the diversity of the students in the classroom. Every student's work, efforts, and accomplishments should be displayed and celebrated (Jalongo & Isenberg, 2004). Simple tasks such as posting maps to highlight students' country of origin or displaying signs or banners welcoming students in their own languages can help instill pride (Weinstein, Curran, & Tomlinson-Clarke, 2003).

Accessibility issues should also be in the forefront of your mind when designing spaces inside and outside of the classroom. For example, it's important to ensure that restrooms and drinking fountains are accessible for students with disabilities. Likewise, you may also want to consider providing TDD-compatible telephones and ensuring that all exits, doors, and ramps are accessible.

Creating an Inclusive Community

Although the previously discussed aspects contribute to the general classroom ethos, other factors, such as creating a climate of physical safety and emotional and intellectual safety, are equally important.

Protecting Students' Physical Safety and Preventing Violence

School climates where emotional violence abounds can cause student casualties (Sagarese & Giannetti, 1999). Students who are exposed to constant harassment and mistreatment can become depressed, have eating disorders, and even consider suicide. Sagarese and Giannetti (1999) report, "Adolescent suicide is up 120 percent and one-third of gay, lesbian, and bisexual students [would] rather die than face school." Staggering statistics such as these remind us to be mindful of protecting our students' overall safety.

Within the last 10 years, media reports about shootings in schools have become more prominent. These violent incidents appear to share at least one common theme—the perpetrators were isolated. These students were often alienated from the school fabric and harbored feelings of rejection, humiliation, and rage. Sagarese and Giannetti (1999) speak of a growing number of schools that can be characterized by their climate of cruelty. For many middle and high schools, there is a "hidden curriculum" of "humiliation and intimidation." In these schools, students often face common injustices and trials such as shunning, being shunned, and scapegoating. Students who are not part of the mainstream often encounter verbal abuse, vicious name calling, and physical abuse. The greatest brunt seems to fall on students suspected of being or identified as homosexual, lesbian, or bisexual. Both genders are subject to being bullies, becoming bullied, or becoming part of the silent majority who become desensitized (Sagarese & Giannetti, 1999).

Students with learning and behavior problems appear to be especially susceptible to harassment and bullying. When students are isolated from the general student population because they attend classes with other special needs students, there is an increased risk for being bullied (Hooker & Salk, 2003, in Vaughn & Bos, 2009). Unfortunately, too many teachers do not think there is a real problem with bullying and do not intercede. Bullying tends to escalate at the middle school level (Vaughn & Bos, 2009).

Secondary students often have many tasks to manage. Thorson (2003) reports that "adolescents must develop new and more mature relationships with their peers, achieve and accept socially responsible behavior, accept their physical appearance, accept a sex role, become emotionally and economically independent from their parents, prepare for marriage and family life, and acquire an ideology and value system" (Havighurst & Klaczynski, 1990, cited in Thorson, 2003, p. 87).

Protecting both male and female students from sexual harassment is another concern we must address. Sagarese and Giannetti (1999) define sexual harassment as "any word or action sexual in nature that makes the recipient feel embarrassed and degraded." They also provide the following suggestions for addressing sexual harassment with your students. First, inform your students about what sexual harassment is and tell them that sexual harassment has no place in the classroom or in school. Second, reassure students that reporting such behavior is not tattling. Inform them of their responsibility to report these behaviors as members of a democratic community. Third, encourage students' idealism and activism and empower them to create school projects that provide opportunities for them to understand and become more proactive about sexual harassment. Finally, reach out to parents and let them know the importance of supporting this issue at home.

Protecting Students' Intellectual Safety

Students' intellectual safety addresses their right to be who they are and express themselves without fear of ridicule or failure. Students who are empowered feel comfortable and confident about expressing themselves or their point of view respectfully, even if the teacher has an opposing viewpoint. All students should have the right to search for meaning in the learning process and have their cultural identity represented and valued in the instructional process and the curriculum. Teachers have a major role in modeling appreciation for each individual's differences and making sure that every student facilitates the success of the whole group.

Another important aspect of nurturing intellectual safety is helping students recognize that "fair" doesn't necessarily mean "same" or "equal." Fair should mean that everyone gets what he or she needs. This concept undergirds practices such as differentiated assignments and supplementary behavior management tools like behavioral contracting. Students must be taught to respect and appreciate learning and behavioral differences in order for a differentiated classroom to work.

Can This Work in My Setting?

Depending upon your teaching context, you may feel that the ideas we discussed are unattainable in your particular school setting. We are not so naïve as to suggest that these principles can occur without a great deal of self-examination, self-efficacy, and professional development. Most important, we would like to underscore the vital importance of the persistent, reflective work of teachers. Experienced teachers know that how students perceive their classroom climate influences their overall academic success. The importance of student buy-in can neither be discounted nor overestimated.

To help you reap satisfying results in your classroom, Kellough and Carjuzaa (2006) offer four suggestions. First, your students must feel that the classroom environment supports their efforts. Second, your students must sense that you care about their learning and that they are welcome in your classroom. This is true for most students, regardless of the level of education. Third, students must understand that although the expected learning will be challenging, it is not impossible for them to achieve. High expectations accompanied by culturally sensitive supportive measures are critical elements of a successful plan. Without appropriate teacher support, high expectations for students are empty demands. Finally, your students must realize that the anticipated learning outcomes in your classroom are worth their time and effort to achieve. Students need reassurance that what we expect from them and the intended consequences are worthwhile. As educators, it behooves us to embed that understanding and link that practical knowledge to our instructional delivery. Let's revisit Ms. Smith and take a look at how she helps Victor get acclimated to her classroom.

As Ms. Smith welcomes Victor to her classroom, she realizes that he may not feel connected to the school. She is concerned that he may be experiencing social alienation. Immediately, she makes a point to greet him before class and have him sit next to a student who will be a peer tutor. After class, Ms. Smith takes a couple of minutes to review key information with him. Ms. Smith places a map of Eastern Europe on the classroom wall that includes the Ukraine and she lets Victor circle his birth city. Every week, she asks Victor to share a word in his first language and post it in the classroom with the accompanying meaning. Knowing that Victor enjoys soccer, she also contacts both soccer coaches and identifies a couple of English and social studies honor students on the teams to tutor Victor during their study period. Ms. Smith helps Victor create a journal and encourages him to write what he is experiencing and what he is thinking. She lets him know that she will read it once a week and he will receive course credit for it. Before tests, she reviews the study guide with all students and meets with Victor individually to discuss the material and create graphic organizers to help him understand. Ms. Smith encourages him to review the graphic organizers independently and with his tutors. She speaks with Victor's mother about his participation on the soccer team. Having already spoken to the coaches, Ms. Smith reassures her that he does not have to attend every practice or game because he spends much of his time studying and working a part-time weekend job. Ms. Smith begins to notice that Victor is talking more and has developed relationships with soccer team members and math classmates. He has started speaking more in groups and occasionally will offer a response during whole-group class discussions.

Teachers who care about their students spend time with them. They often go the extra mile to ensure that their students are getting what they need to be successful. They strive to create a learning environment that is safe and protects students from avoidable harm (Kauchak & Eggen, 2003).

How Should I Proceed?

Leading your class in a discussion about the kind of learning environment that would allow them to feel safe and productive would be a wonderful starting point for creating class guidelines. Constellation Community Middle School (CCMS) in Long Beach, California created five core school principles that the entire student body recites daily. The principles are as follows:

1. Anything that hurts another person is wrong.
2. We are each other's keepers.

3. I am responsible for my own actions.

4. I take pride in myself.

5. Leave it better than when you found it. (Kellough & Carjuzaa, 2006, p. 68)

Although most teachers would probably agree with the principles from CCMS, teachers in inclusive classrooms without a collaborative teacher or special education aide need additional strategies and procedures to help them manage and instruct students with behavioral difficulties. The resources at the end of the chapter will be helpful as you move forward with enhancing the environment of your classroom.

• • •

Ultimately, the success of the classroom learning environment begins and ends with you. As you build your learning environment, examine and confront any personal beliefs, attitudes, values, and fears that may interfere with your goals. By doing this self-examination, the potential is there for you to acknowledge and celebrate your personal strengths as well as those of your students (Thorson, 2003). We also recommend the following guidelines for creating a welcoming classroom environment:

- **Acknowledge the importance of infusing an affirming attitude into your classroom climate**—Look for the good and positive things that your students do and give them verbal encouragement.
- **Develop sociocultural competence**—Seek to become more knowledgeable about your students' culture and community.
- **Refine your collaborative skills**—Developing your knowledge about your students will help you bolster your communication skills with parents, the community, and your colleagues.
- **Hone your pedagogy for diversity skills**—The more skills, strategies, and techniques you master, the greater the impact you will have with your students (Voltz, Collins, Patterson, & Sims, 2008).

- **Remember your actions toward your students**—Your actions, both verbal and nonverbal, will signal what you really think about your students' worth and their chances of achieving success.
- **Affirm your own gifts, talents, and sources of inspiration**—Be kind to yourself and acknowledge your strengths. Allow yourself to celebrate small measures of success on your journey.

Highly resilient teachers understand what they must do to create effective learning environments and remain healthy and strong in the profession.

Resources for Creating an Environment of Instruction

BOOKS

Colvin, G. (2004). *Managing the cycle of acting-out behavior in the classroom.* Arlington, VA: CEC.

Crimmins, D., Farrell, A. F., Smith, P. W., & Bailey, A. (2007). *Positive strategies for students with behavior problems.* Baltimore: Brookes.

Cushman, K. (2003). *Fires in the bathroom: Advice for teachers from high school students.* New York: The New Press.

Kapalka, G. (2009). *8 steps to classroom management success: A guide for teachers of challenging students.* Thousand Oaks, CA: Corwin.

Mather, N., & Goldstein, S. (2008). *Learning disabilities and challenging behaviors: A guide to intervention and classroom management.* Baltimore: Brookes.

Waller, R. J. (2009). *The teacher's concise guide to functional behavior assessment.* Thousand Oaks, CA: Corwin.

JOURNAL ARTICLES

Bondy, E., Ross, D. D., & Gallingane, C. (2007). Creating classroom environments of success and resilience: Culturally responsive classroom management and more. *Urban Education, 42,* 326–348.

Cartledge, G., Singh, A., & Gibson, L. (2008). Practical behavior-management techniques to close the accessibility gap for students who are culturally and linguistically diverse. *Preventing School Failure, 52(3),* 29–38.

Curran, M. E. (2003). Linguistic diversity and classroom management. *Theory into Practice, 42,* 334–340.

Duhaney, L. M. (2003). A practical approach to managing the behaviors of students with ADD. *Intervention in School and Clinic, 38,* 267–279.

Hendley, S. L. (2007). 20 ways to use positive behavior support for inclusion in the general education classroom. *Intervention in School and Clinic, 42,* 225–228.

Monroe, C. R. (2006). Misbehavior or misinterpretation. *Kappa Delta Pi Record, 42,* 161–165.

Simonsen, B., Sugai, G., & Negron, M. (2008). Schoolwide positive behavior supports: Primary systems and practices. *Teaching Exceptional Children, 40*(6), 32–40.

Soodak, L. (2003). Classroom management in inclusive settings. *Theory into Practice, 42,* 327–333.

Weinstein, C. (2003). Culturally responsive classroom management: Awareness into action. *Theory into Practice, 42*(4), 269–276.

VIDEOS

ASCD. (2004). Classroom management that works. [Video]. Alexandria, VA: Author.

PBS. (2008). The motivation breakthrough. [Video]. Arlington, VA: Author.

WEB SITES

Center for Effective Collaboration and Practice: Functional Behavior Assessment: http://cecp.air.org

Second Step: www.secondstep.org. This site offers an intervention program to reduce bullying.

Positive Behavioral Interventions and Supports: www.pbis.org

10 Take-Away Tips for Social and Emotional Learning: http://www.edutopia.org. This site shows how a school district demonstrates SEL strategies that work.

4

Developing the Content for Instruction

In this chapter, we will discuss the fourth element of the MMECCA framework, the **CONTENT** of instruction. In most contemporary schools, the curriculum is largely shaped by standards from state or local agencies about what students should know or be able to do. As stated by Rakow (2008), "At the dawn of the 21st century in education, it is impossible to talk about teaching, curriculum, schools, or education without discussing standards" (p. 43).

Curricular Challenges in Inclusive Classrooms

As discussed in the Introduction, it seems difficult to balance standardized learning outcomes mandated by standards-based reform with individualized learning outcomes for students with disabilities and students from diverse cultural backgrounds. Again, it is important to remember that the goal of the standards movement is to enhance learning outcomes for all students by setting goals with respect to those outcomes. In other words, standards merely articulate where students will ideally end up, not the route they must take to get there. Customizing that route is where the individualized learning comes in.

It also is important to remember we cannot standardize the rate at which our students move through the curriculum. While different students may be at different points on the learning continuum, they are all moving in the same direction toward accomplishing the same learning goal. It is our challenge to determine where each student falls on the learning continuum and plan the best route to move each student forward.

Aside from student variability, we are often challenged by the breadth of content reflected in the standards that guide our curricula. Some curricula in the United States have been characterized as being "a mile wide and an inch deep" (Schmidt et al., 1999, p. 4). Reeves (2003) attributes this tendency to the process through which states derive standards. According to Reeves (2003), "Every state creates standards based on a political process [that] is a reflection of a sincere desire by state officials to include multiple points of view in the creation of standards" (p. 20). While such an inclusive approach is appropriate and necessary to secure needed buy-in from significant stakeholders, it is likely that this approach also increases the breadth of content. Such breadth may make educators feel rushed to "cover" content at the expense of depth of coverage. While superficial coverage is undesirable for any group of students, it is particularly so for students who may have less background knowledge or who may require an extensive review of the material in order to master the targeted knowledge or skill.

An additional curricular challenge associated with standards-based reform is the inclination to put a "hyper" focus on the standards that serve as the foundation for accountability assessments. When teachers put all of their energy into these standards, they may diminish their attention to other critical elements of the curriculum, such as the arts or multicultural education (Bohm & Sleeter, 2001).

Incorporating Important Curricular Considerations

Given the challenges we discussed above, we must reflect on how we approach issues related to the content of instruction. The following topics represent some of those issues that educators should give special consideration as we plan instructional content for our diverse and inclusive classrooms.

Emphasizing Power Standards

Reeves (2000) argues that one of the biggest threats to the standards movement is the large number of standards that educators are often asked to address. He suggests a more judicious focus on the standards that he refers to as "power standards." Conderman and Bresnahan (2008) refer to this content as "big ideas." Reeves (2000) suggests that we ask ourselves the following three important questions about each standard that undergirds our curricula:

- Does this standard represent knowledge or skill that has enduring importance? In other words, does the standard reflect something that will be important for students to know for years to come? Or is it something that may just reflect a passing trend?
- Does this standard transcend the boundaries of a single content area? Does it have relevance or applicability in more than one subject area? For example, the skill of reading charts and graphs could be applied in the context of almost any subject area.
- Does this standard serve as the basis for later learning? For example, fraction concepts serve as the basis for understanding decimals which are interwoven into science curricula as well.

By concentrating our efforts on standards that satisfy at least one of these criteria, Reeves contends we can maximize the impact of our instruction. This is not to suggest that other standards should be ignored, but rather that standards that reflect big ideas be given special emphasis. Let's revisit Ms. Wilson from Chapter 1 and look at her concerns about incorporating standards into her 3rd grade classroom.

It is the beginning of another school year and Ms. Wilson sees this time as a chance for a fresh start. She looks at the curriculum guide that lists the standards for the first half of the year, and a familiar feeling of frustration begins to surface—so many standards, so little time. Adding to her frustration is the fact that Southside Elementary has been labeled a "school in crisis" because of the school's failure to make adequate yearly progress. Because the pressure is really on Ms. Wilson and her colleagues to increase test scores, she is spending more time preparing to meet with the primary team to plan a course of action. Last year, Ms. Wilson recalls getting bogged down in translations, reflections, and rotations of geometric figures. Ms. Wilson wishes that she had spent more time on fractional concepts because her students will need this skill to build their understanding for concepts later on in the school year. These are some of the issues that she would like to raise with her colleagues at the meeting.

Moving Students Along the Continuum of Skills

Although standards-based reform encourages educators to establish standards to which all students can aspire, we understand that students will move along different paths at different rates as they master these standards. According to Tomlinson (2001), "a student must learn from his or her current point of experience, understanding, and skill" (p. 44). In other words, teachers must be prepared to meet students where they are in order to move them forward. Let's consider how Ms. Wilson incorporates this concept into her classroom.

Ms. Wilson decides to focus more on developing fractional concepts in her instructional sequence. Overall, she is feeling good about her progress with this unit and is beginning to discuss adding like fractions with her class. However, several students in her class, including Dorothy who has mild mental retardation, are still struggling with adding whole numbers. Ms. Wilson will need to revisit the concept of adding whole numbers with these students before they can be expected to understand adding fractional parts and perform the operation accurately.

This scenario reflects the need for content differentiation in standards-based instruction for inclusive classrooms. Ms. Wilson wants Dorothy to master fractional concepts and operations. However, in order for her to reach this goal, she will need to address the prerequisite skills that support it.

In the case of students with disabilities such as Dorothy, standards-based IEPs are developed to align students' individualized learning goals with the established standards. Figure 4.1 outlines a helpful process for establishing this

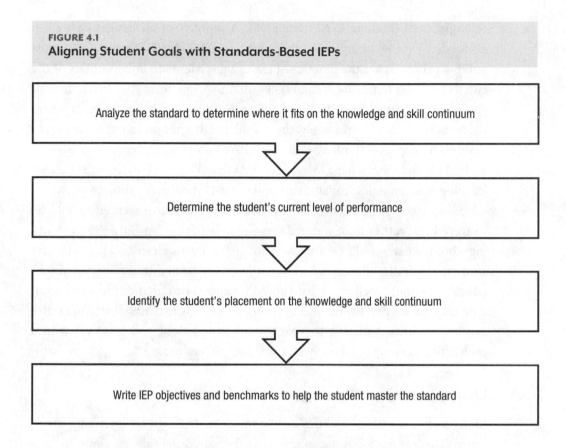

FIGURE 4.1
Aligning Student Goals with Standards-Based IEPs

Analyze the standard to determine where it fits on the knowledge and skill continuum

Determine the student's current level of performance

Identify the student's placement on the knowledge and skill continuum

Write IEP objectives and benchmarks to help the student master the standard

alignment. You can use curriculum guides or scope-and-sequence charts to determine the prerequisite knowledge and skills that support students' mastery of the standard in question. Next, you will need to determine the student's current level of performance relative to this continuum. This process will allow you to determine what knowledge or skills the student may need to master before he or she will be able to reach the targeted standard. Finally, special educators will work with general educators to develop standards-based IEPs.

Watering Up the Curriculum for Students

Quite often for students with disabilities, curricular discussions revolve around eliminating content. The result is often referred to as a "watered down" curriculum. Standards-based reform has encouraged educators to revisit this approach (Malone & Nelson, 2006). A number of challenges have been associated with watering down the curricula (Ellis, 1997). Some of the most notable problems are the practice of exposing students to only portions of the curriculum and removing certain types of knowledge from the curriculum for students with disabilities. These practices diminish the opportunity for these students to learn. Unfortunately, these students are not given opportunities to develop higher-level thinking skills because of an overemphasis on mastering basic skills and memorizing loosely related facts. This kind of decontextualized learning is meaningless for students and inhibits their motivation to learn.

Ellis (1997) suggests that the curriculum in inclusive settings should be "watered up" rather than watered down. He believes that rather than thinking about what should be removed from the curriculum to accommodate students with disabilities and students from culturally diverse backgrounds, educators should focus on what should be added or enhanced to accommodate these students. In the next section, we discuss teaching learning strategies to students, situating the content of instruction, and teaching with a multicultural perspective to "water up" the curriculum.

Using Learning Strategies with Students

Many learners with disabilities need explicit instruction on learning how to learn. Consider the following computer analogy. In order for a computer system to function optimally, the hardware must be intact, the processor must run at a certain speed, and the RAM must have enough memory to perform the tasks at hand. In the analogy, the computer hardware represents the student's learning power, the processor is the speed at which the students can learn, and the RAM is the student's capacity for memory. Some students with disabilities have cognitive deficits that may make it difficult for them to learn information at the same rate as their peers, process certain types of information, or use reasoning skills. They also may have difficulty retaining information in their short-term or long-term memory.

In addition to hardware, a computer system also must have software to perform any task. Without software, a state-of-the-art computer can do nothing. In our analogy, the software represents our learning strategies for students. A student may have an outstanding capacity to learn, but if he or she does not know how to use that capacity, the student will be unable to success-fully complete the task at hand.

Finally, a knowledgeable person must be available to manage the computer system in order for it to be productive. This person also needs to be able to decide what tasks need to be accomplished and which software should be used. A state-of-the art computer and a boatload of software will amount to nothing in the hands of a person who doesn't know how and when to use it. In our analogy, the computer operator represents the student's executive function. Fisher and Happe (2005) have described executive function as "processes responsible for higher level action control, in particular those that are necessary for maintaining a mentally specified goal and for implementing that goal in the face of distracting alternatives" (p. 757). According to Figueras and colleagues (2008)

> The construct of executive function (EF) encompasses the organizational and self-regulatory skills required for goal-directed, nonautomatic behavior. It has been variously described as including planning, initiating, monitoring, and flexibly correcting actions according to feedback; sustaining as well as shifting attention; controlling impulses and inhibiting prepotent but maladaptive responses; selecting goals and performing actions that may not lead to an immediate reward, with a view to reaching a longer term objective; holding information in mind whilst performing a task (working memory); and creatively reacting to novel situations with nonhabitual responses. (p. 363)

In short, executive function helps students regulate and monitor their thinking and behavior. Students who have deficits in this area also often have learning and behavior problems despite their capacity to excel.

Researchers have found that it is useful to explicitly teach learning strategies to students with cognitive challenges. Mercer and Pullen (2005) propose integrating the following types of strategy instruction into the curriculum:

- **Learning Strategy Instruction.** This type of strategy instruction is designed to teach students how to cope with the academic demands encountered at school, home, community, or employment settings. These learning strategies teach students how to respond to critical reading, writing, listening, remembering, and test-taking demands.

- **Social Skill Strategy Instruction.** This type of strategy instruction is designed to teach students how to interact appropriately with others across a variety of situations and settings. Skills such as resisting pressure, accepting criticism, negotiating, following directions, and asking for help are included.
- **Motivation Strategy Instruction.** This type of strategy instruction enables students to become active in planning the direction of their lives. Skills for teaching students how to set, monitor, attain, and communicate goals in important areas of their lives are included.
- **Executive Strategy Instruction.** This type of strategy instruction is designed to teach students how to solve problems independently and generalize learning. Students learn these strategies after they receive instruction in three to five other learning strategies. (p. 174)

Examples of Learning Strategies

Learning strategy instruction helps students remember how to perform academic tasks. The Capitalization, Overall Appearance, Punctuation, and Spelling (COPS) strategy is an example of a learning approach that helps students proofread their work (Schumaker, Nolan, & Deshler, 1991). The acronym COPS is a mnemonic device that students can use to recall the steps for proofreading their work. You can tell students to "watch for the cops" as they proofread their papers. The students will write the letters C-O-P-S at the top of their draft papers and then read through and check the paper for each of the COPS elements. After students review each element, they can check off the corresponding letter. The COPS elements are as follows:

C = **Capitalization.** Students read through their draft papers to check for capitalization errors.

O = **Overall Appearance.** Students review their draft papers to check for overall appearance. For example, students may be asked to use specific margins or spacing.

P = **Punctuation.** Students check their draft papers for punctuation errors.

S = **Spelling.** Students check their draft paper for spelling errors.

TOWER is a learning strategy that students can use for the writing process (Schumaker, Denton, & Deshler, 1984). You can tell students, "When you write, you build a tower." The TOWER elements are as follows:

T = **Think.** Think about what you want to write. Jot down your major points.

O = **Order.** Decide the order you will use when you write down your ideas. For example, will your major points be presented in chronological order, order of importance, or in another order?

W = **Write.** Write a first draft of your paper.

E = **Edit.** Proofread your first draft. You may want to use the COPS strategy.

R = **Rewrite.** Rewrite your draft and incorporate the edits you made in the previous step.

RAP is a learning strategy that students can use for reading comprehension (Schumaker, Denton, & Deshler, 1984). You can tell your students, "When you read, you should be able to rap about it." The RAP elements are as follows:

R = Read a paragraph.

A = Ask yourself about the main idea and details.

P = Put it in your own words.

Students can use the STAR strategy for solving algebra word problems (Gagnon & Maccini, 2001). You can tell your students, "Be an algebra STAR." The STAR elements are as follows:

S = **Search the problem.** Read the problem carefully to determine what you are asked to find.

T = **Translate the words into an equation.** Identify a variable and select an operation. Visualize a concrete representation. Write the equation.

A = **Answer the problem.**

R = **Review the solution.**

Examples of Executive Strategies

Executive strategies are designed to assist students in making appropriate choices and solving problems independently. The FAST strategy is an approach that helps students control impulsive behavior. You can tell students, "To keep out of trouble, you have to think FAST." The FAST elements are as follows:

F = Freeze. Don't react right away. Stop and think first.
A = Alternatives. Consider your choices or alternatives for reacting. Consider the consequences for each choice.
S = Select. Choose the most appropriate action from the alternatives.
T = Try it. Go with your plan.

Mercer and Pullen (2005) suggest the following steps for integrating strategy instruction into the curriculum:

- **Pre-test and assess students' skills.** Before strategy instruction begins, assess the student's current performance level for the skill in question. For example, if you are considering using the COPS approach, look at the student's proofreading skills and determine whether or not the student has the necessary prerequisite skills for this strategy. For the COPS approach, students need to know capitalization and punctuation rules. Before strategy instruction begins, tell students how the strategy will help them.
- **Describe the strategy.** Explain each step of the strategy with students and tell them how they can apply it.
- **Model the strategy.** If you are teaching the COPS strategy to a student, use a draft of the student's work, implement each step in the strategy, and explain as you go through each step.
- **Elaborate and rehearse the strategy.** Describe the purpose of the strategy and its steps with your students. Review the process with your students until they become familiar with the strategy.
- **Provide controlled practice and feedback.** At the beginning, ask your student to use a strategy on less complex material. When you are

teaching the COPS strategy, use a shorter draft of the student's work rather than a long, complex draft. You can prompt the students and provide feedback as they implement the strategy.

- **Provide advanced practice and feedback.** Allow students to use a strategy on more advanced material. Gradually fade the level of cueing and prompting you give to your students.
- **Use post-tests and elicit commitments from students.** Allow students to apply a strategy on more advanced material without giving them coaching and feedback. Celebrate your students' success.
- **Encourage students to think about other ways to use the strategy.** Allow students to discuss other situations in which the strategy can be useful. Ask the students how they plan to remember to use the strategy. Actively monitor and reinforce your students' use of the strategy.

Let's take another look at Ms. Smith and how she applies the COPS strategy with the students in her diverse and inclusive 10th grade English class.

Ms. Smith notices that many of her students do not proofread their papers before turning them in. These papers often have numerous capitalization, punctuation, and spelling errors, even though these students know better. She suspects that they are not focusing on these issues, so she decides to introduce the COPS strategy.

Ms. Smith begins by pointing out to her students that she has noticed inconsistent uses of the capitalization and punctuation rules discussed in class and misspellings of common words that she knows they know how to spell. She shows them examples of work with errors and tells them how often these types of errors occur. Afterward, Ms. Smith discusses why these errors are a problem and cites how they make it difficult for the reader to understand the intended message of the writer.

Next, Ms. Smith introduces the COPS strategy to her students. She explains how she has successfully used this strategy and encourages her students to learn it. Ms. Smith describes each of the steps of the strategy and then demonstrates how to use it with a sample of her own writing that is projected on a screen for the students to see. Ms. Smith writes the letters C-O-P-S across the top of her draft, reads through her draft once looking only for capitalization errors, and uses cognitive modeling (i.e., thinking aloud) to discuss how she applies this step and the kinds of things that she is thinking about. After reading through the draft for capitalization, Ms. Smith places a check mark by the letter C in the acronym COPS. She repeats this step for the O (overall appearance), the P (punctuation), and the S (spelling). Ms. Smith uses questioning to check for her students' understanding as she demonstrates the strategy.

After Ms. Smith models the strategy, she removes her draft from the students' view and asks them to do a fast write on the strategy and outline its purpose and each of the steps. She gives them time to write two paragraphs and write about which steps may be easiest or hardest for them. Meanwhile, Ms. Smith does the same and makes sure that there are some mechanical errors in her draft. Next, she allows her students to orally review the strategy and its steps. Then, she displays her paragraphs to her students.

In order to provide controlled practice and feedback, Ms. Smith asks the students to walk her through the COPS strategy as they proofread her paragraphs. Then, she encourages her students to apply the COPS strategy to proofread their own work. Ms. Smith circulates among her students and gives them coaching and feedback as needed. She individually visits those students who are struggling with proofreading.

On the following day, Ms. Smith allows the students to verbally review the purpose and steps of the COPS strategy. Next, she asks them to apply the strategy to a longer essay that they previously wrote. For this activity the students will work in pairs to support each other in applying the strategy. Afterward, Ms. Smith encourages her students to discuss their experiences in applying the strategy. Her students can discuss what areas were most difficult, how many errors they were able to detect, how they worked together with their partner, and how they think the strategy will help them. At the close of the session, Ms. Smith collects the papers for review and provides feedback to students during the following session.

In subsequent sessions, Ms. Smith will allow her students to apply the COPS strategy independently without her coaching. She will ask the students whether they are applying the strategy in other classes or in non-school activities. Ms. Smith will talk with her colleagues to determine if they've noticed her students using the strategy in their classes. She will note and reinforce instances in which students use the strategy effectively without being explicitly told to do so.

Strategy instruction can be a powerful way of "watering up" the curriculum in diverse classrooms. Both students with and without disabilities can benefit from this approach.

Connecting Students to the Content

Another powerful way to "water up" the curriculum is to connect it to things that are relevant to the learner. Style (1996) argued that the curriculum should serve as both a window and a mirror for students—a window into a world that is different from their own and a mirror that reflects their own image. Because many students often see school learning as foreign to their everyday concerns, it's our challenge to help learners see how what they study in schools is connected to something that is relevant for them. According to Duerr (2008)

> The word "curriculum" is by its own definition a noun: a thing. But that is a flat definition. Isn't the goal of educators everywhere to engage students in what they're learning? Why can't curriculum be transformed into a verb, something dynamic and ever changing, in which ideas, books, and concepts come alive? In the end, curriculum should be not a dusty, brittle list of goals and objectives but a flexible set of relationships and activities that evolve from a group of adults (teachers) and a larger number of young people (students) interacting with a set of resources. (p. 175)

Integrating curriculum is one way to accomplish this goal. Shoemaker (1989) defined an integrated curriculum as "education that is organized in such a way that it cuts across subject-matter lines, bringing together various aspects of the curriculum into meaningful association to focus upon broad areas of study" (p. 5). Personalized contextual instruction is a form of integrated curriculum that blends various content areas and explores student-identified questions related to a given theme (Voltz, 2003). To implement personalized contextual instruction, you can use interest inventories to determine the areas that interest your students and anchor your themes and units around these areas. In an elementary setting, such units can be planned by an individual teacher. In middle and high school settings, these units require team planning based on subject matter. Figure 4.2 displays a sample of personalized contextual instruction in a thematic unit on the Olympics.

Consider how Mr. Thomas outlines the use of personalized contextual instruction in his middle school classroom.

Mr. Thomas and his team have been discussing their students' detachment from what they are learning, their apparent lack of motivation, and their inability to apply the knowledge and skills they learn in school to real-life problem solving. Mr. Thomas suggests that students don't understand the importance of what they learn in school and don't see how the things they learn are related to them. To address these issues, he suggests using integrated instruction and his team embraces this idea.

Mr. Thomas and his team use interest inventories to identify things that are relevant to their students. There has been quite a buzz lately about the Olympics and this event emerges as a topic of interest for many students. Each teacher on the team asks his or her class what they already know about the Olympics and what they'd like to learn. These teachers also invite their students to do an individual fast write and discuss ideas about more of the things they'd like to know. Each teacher records what each class has said about what they know, what they'd like to learn, and how they think they should go about it.

After this information has been collected, Mr. Thomas and the team meet again to see how the students' feedback aligns with the standards for their classes. They decide how they will work together to deliver instruction that is both tied to content standards and anchored in a theme that is relevant to students.

This approach not only taps into student interest, but also shows how the subject areas are interrelated and support each other. This strategy sets the stage for more meaningful learning to occur.

FIGURE 4.2
Sample Personalized Contextual Instruction Chart

Area of Student Interest: The Olympics				
What Students Know	**What Students Would Like to Learn**	**Students' Ideas About How They Can Find Out About This Topic**	**Content Area**	**Related Content Standards**
Athletes from different countries compete in the Olympics	Which countries have won the most Olympic medals?	Conduct research on the Internet Read about the Olympics in books, newspapers, and magazines	Literacy Math Social Studies	Select and indicate preferences for sources to gather information Display information using bar graphs Identify specified countries on the globe Discuss the impact of a country's climate on various sports
The Olympics are held in different parts of the world	What countries have hosted the Olympics most often and in which sports? How and why countries are selected to host the Olympics?	Conduct research on the Internet Read about the Olympics in books, newspapers, and magazines	Literacy Math Science Social Studies	Identify main ideas and supporting details Display information using bar graphs Interpret weather data Examine other environmental characteristics (e.g., pollution) that can impact various types of athletic performance Discuss the impact of significant world events on the Olympics

Infusing Multicultural Perspectives into the Curriculum

Teaching with a multicultural perspective is another way to "water up" the curriculum. Content integration is probably what most people think of when they hear the term "multicultural education." Unfortunately, content integration can be limited by an exclusive focus on what some have termed "the four Fs"—foods, fashions, famous people, and festivals (Gollnick &

Chinn, 2009). While there is nothing inherently wrong in including this content in the curriculum, an exclusive focus on such content reflects a very impoverished view of multi-cultural education and provides only superficial exposure to multicultural concepts. Banks (2001) recommends for teachers to keep the following guidelines in mind as they incorporate multicultural concepts into the curriculum:

* Historical perspectives of diverse groups
* Contemporary experiences of diverse groups in our society
* Contributions of diverse groups
* Language and communication patterns of diverse groups
* Bias reduction
* Skills for intercultural interaction

Youth culture also is an important element to be considered as you include multicultural education into your curriculum. Morrell (2002) recommends educators to attend to several elements of youth culture, such as popular music, television, and film. Additionally, electronic and computer-based tools of youth culture (e.g., Internet, iPods) should also be integrated into instruction.

As important as the content itself is the manner in which this content is infused into the curriculum. When discussions about multicultural content are limited to a particular time of year or to a particular subject area, marginalization of this content occurs. For example, if the contributions of African Americans are discussed only during February, the unintended message to students may be that this is the only time that this content has any relevance. Likewise, if this content is addressed only in the context of a single subject, such as social studies, the message may be that this is the only aspect of the curriculum for which multicultural content has any relevance. While content integration should not be contrived, there are some authentic opportunities to infuse multicultural concepts throughout the curriculum, including areas such as math and science. Consider how the teachers in the next two scenarios infuse multicultural concepts into these lesson plans from Grant and Sleeter (2008).

Mr. Alvarez is a high school science teacher and he is planning a unit on cardiovascular health. His classes are very diverse and include English language learners, students from a variety of cultural backgrounds, and students with learning disabilities. In the past, Mr. Alvarez has taken a very traditional approach to teaching this unit and has used strategies such as lecturing about how the heart and circulatory system work, showing videos, making three-dimensional models, and providing related textbook readings to support these lectures. Mr. Alvarez has also invited a nurse to be a guest speaker and discuss the impact of diet on cardiovascular health. To assess student learning, he used a quiz at the end of the unit.

Because Mr. Alvarez has learned quite a bit about multicultural teaching since he last taught this unit, he decided to make some changes. For example, rather than beginning the unit with a general overview of the cardiovascular system, he starts by asking the students to share their experiences with family members or friends who have heart disease. Mr. Alvarez also decides to incorporate more group activities into the unit. For example, one group will develop and defend an exercise program for youth that promotes cardiovascular health. Another group will analyze menu items from different ethnic restaurants and discuss how these items could be modified to make them more heart healthy. A third group will develop a Spanish-English dictionary that will help Spanish speakers who are learning English communicate with English-speaking doctors about issues related to cardiovascular health. Students will also be divided into groups to explore the contributions of male and female scientists from diverse backgrounds with respect to current understandings and medical interventions related to the cardiovascular system. At the close of the unit, Mr. Alvarez evaluates each student's learning through group presentations and individual quizzes.

Mrs. McKinney is planning a unit on functions for her high school math class. When Mrs. McKinney taught this unit in the past, she discussed related terminology (e.g., domain, range, and rule) and the related symbols. She also used quantities that vary together (e.g., height and weight, income and taxes, time elapsed, and distance traveled) to illustrate to students that they must pay attention to both quantities to understand the relationship. Then, she demonstrated how mathematical equations could be developed to express these relationships. She assessed students' progress through homework assignments and a quiz.

As Mrs. McKinney approaches teaching this unit again, she decides to make some changes based on what she has learned about multicultural teaching. She begins by asking each student to identify at least four popular musicians and describe the length of their careers, the number of songs recorded, and the number of songs they had to reach the top 40. After this information has been collected, her students will create a table that lists the number of songs the artist recorded and number of songs that reach the top 40. Then, Mrs. McKinney presents the idea that these relationships also can be represented in mathematical terms. This concept becomes the entry point into the unit, and she can teach students to write formulas that represent various aspects of the musicians' careers. She closes the unit by assessing students' mastery of the concepts through oral presentations, homework, and quizzes.

Both of these scenarios illustrate how multicultural content can be infused into subjects that are not generally considered an intuitive fit for this content. Incorporating content about the contributions of diverse groups (e.g., diverse scientists and musicians), as well as the language of diverse groups (e.g., Spanish-English dictionary) has enhanced these lessons. Tapping into youth culture also is an important element of multicultural education that can be seen in these lessons (e.g., functions related to popular musicians). These elements serve as a powerful means of "watering up" the curriculum. They also provide important "windows and mirrors" into the curriculum that facilitate the learning of diverse students.

Bias reduction is another important element of multicultural curricula. This concept focuses on reducing the extent to which students prejudge other individuals based on race, ethnicity, gender, age, disability status, language, or other factors. Bias reduction is an aspect of the curriculum that does not necessarily need to be taught through stand-alone lessons. Consider how the teachers in the next two scenarios reduce bias in their classrooms based on lesson plans from the Southern Poverty Law Center's *Teaching Tolerance* magazine.

Mr. Adams is exploring ways to introduce the concept of bias to students in his 1st grade class. After careful thought, he decides to use a simulation. He instructs half of the class to put a green sticky dot on their palms; the other half will use a blue sticky dot. Mr. Adams makes sure that his students can see the color of the sticky dots for each of their classmates. Next, he proceeds with his class discussion as usual. During the discussion, Mr. Adams only calls on the students who have blue sticky dots. After students have sufficient time to observe and discuss the pattern, he asks students if they notice something that doesn't seem right. At this point, he introduces the concept of bias. He asks students with green dots how it felt to be ignored. Mr. Adams discusses how a teacher's bias might affect student behavior if the teacher were to continue with the same pattern.

Ms. Chen is required to use the state-adopted text for instruction in her high school social studies class. One of the weaknesses in the text is the lack of women in historical events. Ms. Chen decides to use this weakness as a learning opportunity. After completing a unit on 20th century American history, she asks her students to review the chapter and make two separate lists for the names of males and females included in the chapter. When her students find only one or two females mentioned, she asks why this may be the case. Ms. Chen encourages them to think about who decides what is important enough to get into a textbook and how information gets passed down over time. She discusses which voices are more likely to be heard and which voices are more likely to be silenced. Ms. Chen talks with her class about how information from a textbook can shape their worldview and can perpetuate the status quo. She supplements her conversation with information about significant female contributors.

The previous scenarios illustrate how bias reduction can be integrated into the existing curriculum. This approach allows teachers to address traditional curricular content while infusing multicultural concepts.

• • •

The content of what is taught in our classrooms is one of the most critical elements in designing effective instruction. In this chapter, we have explored important curricular considerations for teaching in diverse and inclusive settings. These considerations include focusing on power standards, moving students along the continuum of skills, and "watering up" the curriculum through means such as infusing strategy instruction, contextualizing the content, and infusing multicultural concepts. The key idea is to structure the content of instruction in ways that respond to students' learning characteristics while still addressing established content standards.

The following chapter will expand on these ideas and provide ways that educators can work with parents, families, and each other to build and deliver educational programs that meet the needs of diverse learners.

Resources for Learning Strategy Instruction

BOOKS

Minskoff, E., & Allsopp, D. (2003). *Academic success strategies for adolescents with learning disabilities and ADHD*. Baltimore: Brookes.

Reid, R., & Lienemann, T. O. (2006). *Strategy instruction for students with learning disabilities*. New York: Guildford Press.

JOURNAL ARTICLES

Farenga, S., Ness, D., & Flynn, G. (2007). Strategies for learning and metacognition: Identifying and remembering big ideas. *Science Scope, 31*(2), 82–88.

Kleinheksel, K. A., & Summy, S. E. (2003). Enhancing student learning and social behavior through mnemonic strategies. *Teaching Exceptional Children, 36*(2), 30–35.

McClanahan, B. (2008). Help! I have kids who can't read in my world history class! *Preventing School Failure, 53*(2), 105–111.

WEB SITES

Kansas University Center for Research on Learning: www.kucrl.org. This site features a variety of materials related to learning strategies.

LD Online: www.ldonline.org. This site contains examples of learning strategies for students with learning disabilities.

Resources for Contextualized Instruction

BOOKS

Drake, S. M. (2007). *Creating standards-based integrated curriculum: Aligning curriculum, content, assessment, and instruction.* Thousand Oaks, CA: Corwin Press.

Fogarty, R. J., & Stoehr, J. (2007). *Integrating curricula with multiple intelligences: Teams, themes, and threads.* Thousand Oaks, CA: Corwin Press.

Johnson, E. B. (2001). *Contextual teaching and learning: What it is and why it's here to stay.* Thousand Oaks, CA: Corwin Press.

Ronis, D. L. (2008). *Clustering standards in integrated units.* Thousand Oaks, CA: Corwin Press.

JOURNAL ARTICLES

McComas, W. F. (2009). Thinking, teaching, and learning science outside the boxes. *The Science Teacher, 76*(2), 24–28

Uy, F., & Frank, C. (2004). Integrating mathematics, writing, and literature. *Kappa Delta Pi Record, 40,* 180–182.

Voltz, D. L. (2003). Personalized contextual instruction. *Preventing School Failure, 47,* 138–143.

Williams, G. J., & Reisberg, L. (2003). Successful inclusion: Teaching social skills through curriculum integration. *Intervention in School and Clinic, 38,* 206–210.

Resources for Multicultural Education

BOOKS

Banks, J. (2007). *An introduction to multicultural education.* Boston: Allyn and Bacon.

Gay, G. (2000). *Culturally responsive teaching: Theory, research, and practice.* New York: Teachers College Press.

Gay, G. (2003). *Becoming multicultural educators: Personal journey toward professional agency.* Hoboken, NJ: Jossey-Bass.

Grant, C. A., & Sleeter, C. E. (2007). *Doing multicultural education for achievement and equity.* New York: Routledge.

Grant, C. A., & Sleeter, C. E. (2008). *Turning on learning: Five approaches for multicultural teaching plans for race, class, gender, and disability.* Hoboken, NJ: Wiley.

Howard, G. R. (2006). We *can't teach what we don't know: White teachers, multiracial schools.* New York: Teachers College Press.

Takaki, R. (2008). *A different mirror: A history of multicultural America.* Bel Air, CA: Back Bay Books.

JOURNAL ARTICLES

Bruch, P. L., Jehangir, R. R., Jacobs, W. R., & Ghere, D. L. (2004). Enabling access: Toward multicultural developmental curricula. *Journal of Developmental Education, 27*(3), 12–19; 41.

DomNwachukwu, C. S. (2005). Standards-based planning and teaching in a multicultural classroom. *Multicultural Education, 13*(1), 40–44.

Meyer, C. F., & Rhoades, E. K. (2006). Multiculturalism: Beyond food, festival, folklore, and fashion. *Kappa Delta Pi Record, 42*(2), 82–87.

Van Garderen, D., & Whittaker, C. (2006). Planning differentiated, multicultural instruction for secondary inclusive classrooms. *Teaching Exceptional Children, 38*(3), 12–20.

JOURNALS AND MAGAZINES

International Journal of Multicultural Education: http://ijme-journal.org/index.php/ijme [electronic journal]

Multicultural Education published by Caddo Gap Press

Multicultural Perspectives published by Routledge

Teaching Tolerance published by the Southern Poverty Law Center

PROFESSIONAL ORGANIZATIONS AND CENTERS

National Association for Multicultural Education
5272 River Rd.
Suite 430
Bethesda, MD 20816
www.nameorg.org

Southern Poverty Law Center
400 Washington Ave.
Montgomery, AL 36104
www.splcenter.org

5

Bringing Collaboration into the Classroom for Instruction

In the Introduction, we noted that one of the promises of standards-based reform is to be a catalyst for promoting collaboration between teachers in general education, special education, and ESL and bilingual education. Marilyn Friend and Lynn Cook (2007), noted authors in the field of collaboration for education professionals, define interpersonal collaboration as "a style for direct interaction between at least two co-equal parties voluntarily engaged in shared decision making as they work toward a common goal" (p. 7). Specifically, they describe collaboration as an activity that

- Is voluntary between participants
- Requires parity among participants
- Is based on mutual goals
- Depends on shared responsibility for participation and decision making
- Encourages participants to share resources
- Encourages participants to share accountability for outcomes

Standards-based classrooms with diverse student and teacher populations will include a broad range of individuals. Both teachers and students can benefit from more collaboration within groups. In this chapter, we will discuss the fifth element of the MMECCA framework, **COLLABORATING** for instruction.

Analyzing the Nature of Educational Collaboration

Are all teachers collaborating voluntarily? No. We know that there are some teachers who do not wish to collaborate with others but do so because of legislative mandates, school district policies, or their principal's structure for their specific school environment. If this is the case, is this true and pure collaboration? Probably not. For students, there will be different outcomes based on the level and depth of collaboration between educational professionals. True collaboration requires that the defining characteristics from the previous list are present.

Parity is another issue that causes concern for some teachers when they look at collaboration. Members of a collaborative team may achieve parity when discussing a specific situation, participating in a specific task, or seeking a potential solution for a student. However, when the team members leave that activity, they may revert to job roles that no longer promote parity among the group. The remaining characteristics of collaboration also require that teachers are committed to making every collaborative process successful. Having mutual goals, taking responsibility for participation and decision making, sharing resources, and being accountable for every outcome demand that teachers set aside time to work and plan together.

Allocating and Scheduling Time for Collaboration

As educators, we need support from our administrators to purposefully allocate and schedule planning time for collaboration during the scheduled workday. One of the mistakes that teachers in collaborative groups often make is volunteering their time before or after school, during lunch, or during the weekend. Scheduling time for planning outside of the regular school day is never a satisfactory long-term solution. Teachers will always have obligations to other commitments in the home, family, and community. These competing obligations can create friction in the group or cause team members to question each other's loyalty to the group. Other ways to implement time for collaboration include using creative scheduling concepts, supplemental pay suggestions, and professional development credit options.

Gathering teachers together to collaborate on student outcomes is a multidimensional challenge. Teachers will ask, "What should be done to create purposefully designed planning and collaboration?" "Who needs to be included?" "What groups or subgroups need to have time for collaboration?" and "What are the "soft" factors that need to be considered for diverse students when we plan for collaboration?" Today's schools are environments of change. Children of color are now the majority of students in a number of states and urban areas (Lustig & Koestner, 2006; National Center for Education Statistics, 2007). Many languages other than English are the primary home language for approximately 19 percent of the U.S. population under the age of 5 (U.S. Census Bureau, 2007). The astounding factor for our diverse student population is that the same representation does not exist in the ranks of teachers. Almost 90 percent of general and special education teachers are white (Boyer & Mainzer, 2003). We need to focus on creating collaborative groups that include diverse teachers in our increasingly diverse schools. These collaborative groups can use insights from diverse faculty members to support a greater understanding of the depth of cultural issues and promote growth in cultural sensitivity. Let's look at how the teachers at Ridgeway Middle School address including diverse faculty members in the collaborative teams.

Ms. West, Mr. Barnes, Ms. Hernandez, and Mr. Ashcock teach 6th grade at Ridgeway Middle School, a large inner-city school of 1,000 6th, 7th, and 8th grade students. Eighty-five percent of the student population consists of minority students. Due to the large number of students, each grade is organized in multiple pods with four core teachers who are responsible for each group of students. In Pod 6A, additional teachers and resource personnel work with the students as needed. Ms. West, the language arts teacher, and Mr. Barnes, the science teacher, are in the first three years of their teaching careers. They have strong technology skills and often suggest many new ideas from their teacher education programs. Ms. Hernandez, the math teacher, and Mr. Ashcock, the social studies teacher, have been at Ridgeway for more than 10 years. Ms. Hernandez has strong ties to Ridgeway. She is a member of the community, and she attended the school as a teen. Mr. Ashcock is a dependable member of the faculty. He arrives on time each day, teaches his classes, and leaves campus right on time. He does everything that is asked of him and volunteers for nothing. He rarely speaks up during faculty meetings and has developed no close friendships within the faculty, although he is generally liked by everyone. The students in Pod 6A also receive support from Ms. Jackson, the special education teacher who works with inclusion students in this pod, and Ms. Gabriel, the ESL teacher for 6th grade. There are 110 children in this pod. Thirty-two students are of Latin heritage, 53 are African American, and 25 are white. Ms. Hernandez is the only minority member of the Pod 6A team. She provides an insight into the culture of the neighborhood that carries over into the culture of Ridgeway.

Administrators at Ridgeway are committed to supporting collaboration in the school. They realize that the teachers in Pod 6A need time to plan together, and they allow them to schedule and designate one lunch plus a lunch with extended time as a planning period each week for collaboration. Each team member discusses students who have challenges and revisit each student's progress each week. However, this is just the beginning of teachers' collaborative needs. The entire 6th grade faculty, the 6th grade language arts teachers, the language arts teachers from all three grades, and the special education teachers across the school all need time to collaborate. These groups need time together to continue to grow.

Is it possible to schedule time for each group? Yes. Does it require flexibility? Absolutely. How can teachers stay in touch and keep moving the benefits of their collaboration forward for their students throughout the week? Let's take a look at how technology can foster collaboration.

Using Technology to Create and Extend Collaboration Opportunities

Technology can be part of the solution for creating synchronous and asynchronous collaboration opportunities for teachers. Synchronous communication, such as chat rooms, occurs between parties at the same time. With chat rooms, participating parties can log into a Web site and share their ideas. Some phones are now capable of connecting to interactive sites that contain chat room capabilities. Other examples of synchronous communication are conference telephone calls and camera-to-camera tools like Skype that allow all parties to hear and see each other live. The benefit of using technology-based communication tools is that they provide a vehicle for collaborative activities without requiring everyone to be at the same physical location at the same time. Additionally, some synchronous communication tools archive your communication or provide a transcript from the meetings that users can review later.

Asynchronous communication occurs between parties at different times. One person writes or sends a message when they have time and the person who receives it responds when they are available. The advantages of asynchronous communication are that everyone does not have to be at the same physical location and each person can contribute ideas on different time schedules. Similar to some synchronous communication programs, asynchronous communication also provides a "written record" of the communication. The main disadvantage of asynchronous communication is that the pace of ideas is interrupted by the delays incurred through flexible pacing. It takes longer for everyone to respond and decision making can be delayed. Blogging and wikis are currently some of the most popular asynchronous technologies that can be used for this purpose.

Using Teacher-to-Teacher Collaboration: Co-Teaching in Diverse, Inclusive Classrooms

In our experience, we've seen some classrooms where teachers are supposedly using a co-teaching model, but in reality these classrooms are merely a space where more than one teacher is working. There is no heterogeneous grouping of the students, no co-planning (which is different from just sharing lesson plans), and no joint responsibility for the achievement of all students in the class. The challenge for teachers is to bring collaboration into the co-teaching environment and share the responsibility for the progress of every student. At Ridgeway Middle School, this shared goal would be in place for all 1,000 students at this school, including the 110 students in Pod 6A.

As we take another look at the teachers in Pod 6A, we see that all six teachers possess a variety of skills and information. Including special education and ESL teachers on the teaching team in diverse, inclusive classrooms has become a reality for many schools. By including these teachers on the co-teaching team, each member will have a skilled, supportive, and collaborative team that will enhance the learning environment for all students. Figure 5.1 shows expanded models for co-teaching that you can use in your classroom.

Using Collaboration to Promote Family Involvement in Diverse, Inclusive Schools

Another important role for educators is collaborating with the parents and families of their students. Research has shown a positive link between parental involvement and student learning outcomes (Fan, 2001). Promoting parent involvement is important for all learners, particularly those students who are at risk. Unfortunately, it is often these students with whom educators struggle most in cultivating positive home-school partnerships. According to a report from the National Center for Education Statistics (1998), as poverty levels increase, parent participation in activities such as parent-teacher conferences, open houses, and other events decreases. Likewise, families whose language and cultural backgrounds vary from those of the dominant society sometimes have diminished home-school relationships (National Center for Education Statistics, 2006).

Overcoming Barriers to Effective Home-School Collaborations

There are a number of factors that increase the complexity of promoting strong home-school partnerships with diverse families. Socioeconomic

(text continued on p. 101)

FIGURE 5.1
The Advantages and Disadvantages of Selected Co-Teaching Practices

KEY:

ᵀ̇ General Education Teacher		✖ Typical Learner	
ᵀ̇ Special Education Teacher		✖ Student with Special Needs	
ᵀ̇ ESL Teacher		✖ ELL Student	

INTERACTIVE TEACHING MODELS

Team Teaching	One to Teach, One to Observe	One to Teach, One to Support
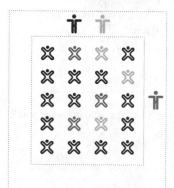	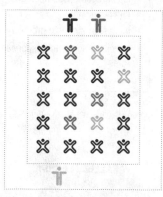	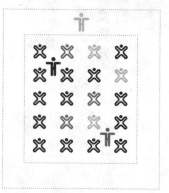
One class of 20 students with one general education teacher, one special education teacher, and one ESL teacher sharing teaching duties.	One class of 20 students with one general education teacher teaching and one special education teacher and one ESL teacher observing the classroom.	One class of 20 students with one general education teacher and one special education teacher teaching and one ESL teacher supporting the students.

Advantages	Disadvantages
• Provides systematic observation and data collection • Promotes role and content sharing • Facilitates individual assistance for students • Models appropriate academic, social, and help-seeking behaviors • Teaches students to ask questions • Provides clarification for students (e.g., concepts, rules, and vocabulary)	• May be just simply "job sharing," and not enriching learning for students • Requires considerable planning • Requires modeling and role-playing skills • Becomes easy to "typecast" a specialist with this role

(continued on next page)

FIGURE 5.1

The Advantages and Disadvantages of Selected Co-Teaching Practices *(con't)*

┌─────────────────────────────── STATION TEACHING ───────────────────────────────┐

Station Teaching

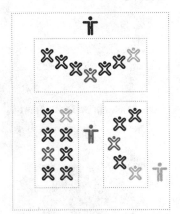

Advantages	Disadvantages
• Provides an active learning format for students • Increases small-group attention • Encourages cooperation and independence • Allows for strategic grouping • Increases students' response rates	• Requires considerable planning and preparation • Increases noise level in the classroom • Requires group and independent work skills • Is difficult for teachers to monitor

One class of 20 students is divided into three stations with one general education teacher, one special education teacher, and one ESL teacher teaching at each station.

┌─────────────────────────────── PARALLEL TEACHING ───────────────────────────────┐

Parallel Teaching

Advantages	Disadvantages
• Provides an effective format for reviewing content with students • Encourages students to respond • Reduces pupil-teacher ratio for group instruction and review	• Each group may not cover the content as equally or as in-depth • May be difficult to coordinate the teaching schedule with another teacher • Requires monitoring of partner pacing • Increases noise level in the classroom • Encourages some teacher-student competition

One class of 20 students is divided into two stations with one special education teacher and one ESL teacher simultaneously teaching at each station.

FIGURE 5.1
The Advantages and Disadvantages of Selected Co-Teaching Practices *(con't)*

--- ALTERNATIVE TEACHING ---

Alternative Teaching

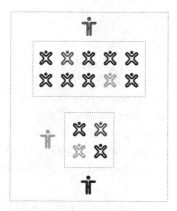

Advantages	Disadvantages
• Facilitates enrichment oppor-tunities for students who need additional help • Offers absent students time to catch up • Keeps individual students and the whole class on pace • Offers time to develop missing skills for students who need additional help	• May be too easy to select or single out the same low-achieving student for help • Creates segregated learning environments • Is difficult to coordinate • Students may feel singled out

One class of 20 students is divided into two stations with teaching and support from one general education teacher, one special education teacher, and one ESL teacher. Students who need more help will receive additional support from teachers at one designated station as needed.

Adapted from *Collaboration for inclusive education* (p. 190) by C. Walther-Thomas, L. Korinek, V. McLaughlin, and B. Williams, 2000, Needham Heights, MA: Allyn & Bacon and *Teaching in today's inclusive classrooms: A universal design for learning approach* (p. 142) by R. Gargiulo and D. Metcalf, 2010, Belmont, CA: Wadsworth. Adapted with permission.

---

factors can negatively influence the development of partnerships between teachers and parents. The fact that people of color are disproportionately represented among our nation's poor often means that these families must spend a greater proportion of their time and energy to meet basic survival needs. In some instances, these families may feel overwhelmed with activities related to their day-to-day survival. Let's take another look at Mr. Jones's student LaMont and his family from Chapter 1.

LaMont is an 11-year-old African American male who is a 6th grader in Mr. Jones's class. He lives with his mother and two older sisters, ages 12

and 14. LaMont's mother, Ms. Drakes, is 31 and currently unemployed. She did not complete high school and has had difficulty securing employment. The family lives in a small apartment in a high-crime area. Their home has been broken into on three separate occasions over the past year. During the same period, Ms. Drakes was robbed at gunpoint while waiting to catch a bus to follow up on a job lead. These events have been emotionally and financially devastating to the family. The family often has to go without utilities or telephone service. It has been a struggle for Ms. Drakes just to keep the family fed, clothed, and safe from physical harm.

Early in his school career, LaMont was classified as a student with emotional disturbance because of his aggressive behaviors toward his classmates and school personnel. Ms. Drakes was taken aback by this placement because she didn't view LaMont's behaviors as extreme. She always taught him not to let others run over him, no matter who they are. Nevertheless, she agreed to the classification. Ms. Drakes did attend a related meeting about LaMont's status, but she didn't fully understand everything that was said. She was intimidated by the educators in the room and the technical language they used. Her contribution to the discussion was minimal. She felt that the educators weren't really interested in what she thought anyway, and she hasn't bothered to attend any other meetings.

With circumstances like these, it's not hard to imagine that families like the Drakes may not always participate as consistently in parent involvement activities as educators or parents themselves may desire. Lack of participation, however, does not mean that parents don't care. When educators are quick to conclude that parents aren't concerned about their child's education, we often engage in thoughts and actions that are counterproductive to our efforts. For example, educators may believe that families who are highly visible in school activities are concerned about the welfare of their children and want to be involved in their education, and they might assume that parents who are not as active do not have similar concerns or desires. Based on these notions, educators may make greater efforts to involve those parents who they assume are concerned, put more value on their contributions and criticisms, and make minimal efforts toward those parents who they assume do not care. Consequently, the differences in the way that "concerned parents" respond to the school versus how "unconcerned parents" respond could be based on how the school interacts with them. This self-fulfilling prophecy can apply to families in the same way that it applies to students.

Breaking the "One-Size-Fits-All" Approach with Students and Their Families

Another barrier that we have as educators in developing positive home-school collaborations is using a "one-size-fits-all" approach for parent involvement. Often, we unilaterally decide what behaviors constitute desired parent involvement and which individuals should be involved. These behaviors are typically thought of as the standard for how families should interact with school personnel. Families whose structure, cultural frameworks, and life circumstances are similar to those of school personnel may be more likely to embrace these behaviors. However, as cultural dissonance increases, so does the likelihood that families will view behaviors prescribed by school personnel to be untenable or inappropriate.

We also need to consider which family members should be involved in home-school collaborations. Because each family's structure is different, the task of bringing the right family members to the table to develop an effective home-school collaboration is an important step. Extended family members, such as grandparents, aunts, or uncles, may play a significant role in the education and socialization of some children from culturally diverse backgrounds. In some cases, these individuals may be the student's legal guardians. Educators should be aware that they may need to work with individuals other than the student's mother or father.

In addition to considering the family structure, as educators we also need to think about different interaction styles from other cultures. For example, some cultures discourage overt confrontation with authority figures like school personnel. In these instances, family members may seem to agree with suggestions from educators when in reality they do not have the same opinion. Family members may promise to do something that they have no intentions of doing. Additionally, some cultures embrace a very separate view of the role of the school versus the role of the home. In these cases, family members may feel it is intrusive for them to collaborate with school personnel on matters they view as strictly the purview of the school, such as a student's performance or behavior in class. Likewise, families may be uncomfortable with school personnel making recommendations regarding what occurs at home with their children, such as specific recommendations regarding the time or place for homework. In these cases, parents may be offended or confused by what school personnel view as a routine request or exchange of information.

Finally, educators should recognize that the concept of deviant or unacceptable behavior is socially constructed. For example, avoiding eye contact or not initiating conversation with an adult may be considered excessively passive in the dominant culture, but it may be desirable in another culture. Likewise, talking loudly or talking while others are talking might be deemed as rude in the dominant culture, but it may be the preferred interaction style in other cultural groups. Such vast differences in perception can be a source of conflict in collaborative relationships in the classroom when the cultural basis for these differences is not understood.

Recognizing Each Family's Strengths and Needs

One of the most important strategies for addressing cultural barriers between educators and families is differentiating the approach for family involvement based on the strengths and needs of each family. Figure 5.2 presents an adaptation of Kroth and Edge's (2007) Mirror Model of Family Involvement. The model is based on the following assumptions:

- All families have strengths.
- All families have needs.
- All families' strengths and needs differ.
- Although each family's strengths and needs are different, some of these qualities are universal for every family.

FIGURE 5.2
Mirror Model of Family Involvement

		WHAT	HOW
PARENT NEEDS	**FEW**	• Transportation • Child Care • Educational Support (e.g., job skill training, literacy skills, GED preparation, English language skills)	• Refer families to an appropriate community or social service agency • Consider ways to provide these services to families at the school
	SOME	• Training in home-school collaboration skills (e.g., parenting skills, interacting with the school system, and pedagogy)	• Provide families with related videos and readings • Conduct family education groups at school and settings outside the school that are convenient for families
	MOST	• Information on how to suport children's learning at home	• Provide families with related newsletters, notes, calls, e-mails, and videos • Conduct group meetings and individual conferences at school and settings outside the school that are convenient for families
	ALL	• Information regarding school policies and procedures, school and class events, student progress information	• Provide families with related newsletters, notes, calls, e-mails, and videos • Conduct group meetings and individual conferences at school and settings outside the school that are convenient for families
PARENT STRENGTHS	**ALL**	• Special knowledge about children's strengths, needs, and interests • Special knowledge about the family's characteristics, history, and aspirations	• Organize parent conferences at school and settings outside the school that are convenient for families • Conduct telephone interviews and distribute questionnaires to parents
	MOST	• Expertise • Energy • Cultural Knowledge • Time for assistance with or participation in school-related activities	• Provide parent meetings and conferences • Reinforce the importance of school work at home with parents
	SOME	• Expertise • Energy • Cultural Knowledge • Time for assistance with or participation in school-related activities	• Attend ongoing parent training sessions or advisory groups • Encourage parents to spend an hour or more daily assisting students with homework • Encourage parents to serve as a classroom volunteer • Encourage parents to engage in school fundraisers
	FEW	• Expertise • Energy • Cultural Knowledge • Time for assistance with or participation in school-related activities	• Encourage parents to organize and lead parent groups • Encourage parents to serve on curriculum committees or site-based management teams

Adapted from: Kroth, R.L. & Edge, D. (2007). *Communicating with parents and families of exceptional children.* Love Publishing: Denver.

Benefiting from Families' Strengths

In Figure 5.2, we see that most families share a number of important universal strengths and needs. Often, we fail to address these needs and capitalize on each family's strengths. For example, many educators send written letters to students' homes to inform their families about school and classroom policies. Families who have weak literacy skills may not respond well to this approach. An alternate strategy that you can use is to allow students to create videos with important announcements for their families. Students can perform and record skits that focus on critical school or classroom policies and share the videos with their families. If the students are the stars of these videos, family members may be more inclined to watch the videos to see their children perform. Of course, an added benefit of this strategy is that students will become familiar with the policies as they perform their skits.

We also need to remember that the student's family generally has intimate background knowledge about their child's strengths, needs, interests, and aspirations; the family's characteristics and background; and the communities where they live. This information can be invaluable to educators as we plan the best ways to reach and teach our students. You can use parent questionnaires and telephone interviews to access this information. Students can also interview their parents and share this background information with their teachers. It is important that we first establish a level of trust as we work with families by using a collaborative interaction style.

Additionally, if we want family members to share information about themselves, we must be willing to share ourselves as well. The resources section at the end of this chapter includes helpful guidelines for interacting with families. You may discover that some families are willing to assist with school projects or fundraisers, share information about their careers or area of expertise, organize parent groups, or work on school committees or site-based management teams. Some schools have even employed parents to serve as liaisons who assist in translating for families, conducting home visits, and leading parent training groups.

Meeting Families' Needs

Some families may need additional support to gain information about how to facilitate their child's learning at home, get training for parenting skills and health-related services, or access tutors to improve their own literacy skills. While we may not have the expertise or resources to provide these services to families, we should be prepared to refer families to community and social service agencies that can help. Some schools form partnerships with other entities to provide families with full services like health care, GED training, and job coaching. Schools like these are often called full-service community schools or community learning centers. There are approximately 5,000 schools like these in the United States. By providing these types of support systems to families, we can be in a better position to work collaboratively with families to enhance the learning outcomes for their children (Dryfoos, 2008).

We can also meet families' needs by using different locations for group meetings with parents and individual parent conferences. Meeting parents at community centers, local churches, fast food restaurants, grocery stores, or even in their homes may make a difference for some parents who may have had negative school experiences themselves or may feel intimidated or alienated by the school environment. Additionally, hosting events at convenient locations can minimize transportation issues for some parents. If off-site locations are not feasible, school buses could be used during after-school hours to transport groups of parents to the school for individual conferences or group meetings. On-site childcare should also be provided for parents who need it. Finally, remember to invite special education teachers and ESL teachers to parent conferences. These teachers should be an integral part of these discussions. Whenever possible, schedule a joint conference for all of the student's teachers. This practice minimizes the number of conferences that a parent may be asked to attend, allows all stakeholders to be aware of what was said during the conference, and sends the message to parents that the school personnel are working together as a team.

Developing effective collaborative partnerships with families is critical for maximizing educational outcomes for students. Families, regardless of cultural or socioeconomic group, are generally concerned about the educational well-being of their children. It is up to us as educators to find ways to connect with these families and build effective educational partnerships.

Effective collaboration is essential for creating successful inclusive classrooms. As educators, we must carve out time to work together and plan and deliver instruction that meets the needs of our diverse students. We also need to remember to include parents and families and be prepared to differentiate how we work with families as critical members of the team.

Resources for Collaboration

TIPS FOR FINDING TIME FOR COLLABORATION WITH OTHER EDUCATORS

For many teachers and administrators, the lack of adequate time for collaboration presents a barrier to pursuing collaborative activities. The following list includes suggestions for creating shared planning and collaborative discussion time.

1. Combine a common lunch time and preparation period. Teachers and administrators who work together and share a common lunch time and preparation period can use this time for collaboration. When you schedule these time periods together, you can have a 90-minute block of collaboration time.

2. Use planning time allotted outside of the contract day. If you can be paid each month for planning time outside of the contract day, you can use this time period for collaborative activities. You can submit a one-page summary that shows a record of your time and the collaborative decisions made.

3. Record time spent in collaborative activities. Participants in collaborative activities can be given the option of meeting once or twice each month after school (sometimes with other colleagues from their school or with colleagues from several schools). They are not paid for these sessions, but the hours spent problem solving and planning can be applied toward continual professional development credit.

4. Use two-hour release periods for collaborative time instead of professional development days. Instead of using professional development days for large-group workshops, you can use two-hour release periods

throughout the school year for collaborative activities and shared planning.

5. In elementary schools, students can be dismissed 45 minutes early once each week to allow teachers to have joint planning time. The instructional time from this 45-minute period can be added to other school days.

6. In grade-level teams at elementary schools, if you are required to meet for 90 minutes each week to coordinate instruction, make sure that the special educator for each grade level is released for at least 45 minutes to attend this meeting so that co-teaching needs can be addressed.

7. In larger schools, fine and related arts staff members can work with teachers to arrange their schedules and allow them to receive a half day for collaboration time every two or three weeks.

8. In alternative high schools when classes are typically scheduled from 7:30 a.m. to 3:30 p.m., teachers can use the additional time from this type of schedule for collaboration.

9. Use e-mail and Web sites for communication. To supplement face-to-face time, you can use e-mail and Web sites. For example, you can use e-mail to communicate about co-teaching ideas with your team or post lesson plans on a district Web site to share ideas with other teachers.

Adapted from Friend & Cook, 2007.

TIPS FOR ESTABLISHING A CLIMATE OF MUTUAL TRUST AND RESPECT WITH PARENTS

1. **Use titles such as Mr., Mrs., or Ms. when addressing adult family members.** Although using first names may be a way to establish friendly relationships in some cultures, in other cultures it may be condescending or disrespectful. Refrain from addressing adult family members by first name unless you've been specifically invited to do so.

2. **Make sure your initial contact with the family is positive.** Your first interactions with families should focus on something that they

will enjoy hearing, such as a student's accomplishment, a particular strength that you've noticed in the student, or reasons why you are looking forward to working with the student. But remember to be sincere. Only say things that you really believe.

3. **Consider organizing a neutral "getting-to-know-you" event.** You can plan an informal event such as a picnic at a local park or a potluck dinner. If such an event is feasible, it could help to set a positive tone and give you an opportunity to see your students interact with their family members. It may also help to build community among the family members who attend. When planning your event, keep in mind any resource limitations that families may have.

4. **Project an attitude of confidence in family members.** Let families know that you believe that they can and will be viable partners in their child's education. Give them every reason to believe that you know that they care and are important members of the team.

5. **Use language that family members will understand.** Avoid using educational jargon when speaking with family members. Present your ideas to them in everyday language, but avoid being condescending. Your tone of voice, rate of speech, facial expressions, and body language often convey more than the actual words themselves. For example, while it is helpful to explain concepts that may be unfamiliar to family members, doing so in a tone of voice that you usually use with a small child is offensive and sends a counterproductive message to families.

6. **Listen to parents.** Remember that you have as much of an opportunity to learn something useful from families as they do from you. Do not verbally dominate the conversation during your interactions with families. A few moments of silence in the discourse may be needed to invite comments from family members. Directly asking family members what they think or how they feel about something can be useful.

7. **Respect families' concerns.** Even in instances when you feel that the concern is not warranted, don't dismiss it without making an honest attempt to address the issue. If educators do not take families' concerns seriously, then we should not expect for families to take our concerns

seriously, either. For example, if a parent expresses a concern that her son's schoolwork is too difficult, and we ignore this concern because we believe the difficulty level is appropriate, that parent may fail to respond to any concerns that we may have later on. While it may not always be appropriate to acquiesce to families' wishes, it is always appropriate to listen to them with an open mind and try to respond to their needs.

8. **Establish an ongoing rapport with families.** Avoid interacting with families only when crises arise. Interacting with families only when school crises occur does not reflect true collaboration. This behavior signals to the family that they will only hear from you when you deem the school situation to be unmanageable. If we provide adequate quantity and quality interactions with families prior to a crisis, families will likely be more responsive.

9. **Treat family members as individuals.** Although it is helpful to be aware of cultural influences as you develop collaborative relationships with families, resist stereotyping family members based on race, ethnicity, socioeconomic class, or any other characteristic. Recognize that there is more diversity within any particular group than there is between various groups.

Adapted from Voltz, 1994.

Resources for Co-Teaching

BOOKS

Murawski, W. W. (2010). *Collaborative teaching in elementary schools.* Thousand Oaks, CA: Corwin.

Murawski, W. W. (2010). *Collaborative teaching in secondary schools.* Thousand Oaks, CA: Corwin.

JOURNAL ARTICLES

Honigsfeld, A., & Dove, M. (2008). Co-teaching in the ESL classroom. *Delta Kappa Gamma Bulletin, 74*(2), 8–14.

Murawski, W. W., & Dieker, L. (2008). 50 ways to keep your co-teacher: Strategies for before, during, and after co-teaching. *Teaching Exceptional Children, 40*(4), 40–48.

Rice, N., Drame, E., Owens, L., & Frattura, E. M. (2007). Co-instructing at the secondary level: Strategies for success. *Teaching Exceptional Children, 39*(6), 12–18.

Sims, M. J. (2005). If we listen, we might just learn something: Two urban teachers and inclusion. *Focus on Inclusive Education, 3*(1), 1–8.

Resources for Family Involvement

BOOKS

Allen, J. (2007). *Creating welcoming schools: A practical guide to home-school partnerships with diverse families.* New York: Teachers College Press.

Grant, K. B., & Ray, J. A. (2010). *Home, school, and community collaboration: Culturally responsive family involvement.* Thousand Oaks, CA: Sage.

Turner-Vorbeck, T., & Marsh, M. M. (2008). *Other kinds of families: Embracing diversity in schools.* New York: Teachers College Press.

JOURNAL ARTICLES

Colombo, M. W. (2006). Building school partnerships with culturally and linguistically diverse families. *Phi Delta Kappan, 88,* 314–318.

Matuszny, R. M., Banda, D. R., & Coleman, T. J. (2007). A progressive plan for building collaborative relationships with parents from diverse backgrounds. *Teaching Exceptional Children, 39*(4), 24–31.

WEB SITES

The Beach Center: www.beachcenter.org

Middleweb: www.middleweb.com

Power of 2: www.powerof2.org

Blogger: www.blogger.com

Wikispaces: www.wikispaces.com

Skype: www.skype.com

6

Implementing Assessment
for Instruction

In today's diverse classrooms, all learners are expected to meet the stated curricular learning outcomes. Teachers who understand these outcomes and can implement a variety of assessment techniques to reach every student will have a more accurate assessment of each student's knowledge, skills, and dispositions. However, as mentioned in Chapter 1, our students are more diverse than ever and present unique challenges to K–12 teachers. Although we wholeheartedly believe that the diversity that students bring to our schools can be an invaluable resource and asset for teachers, students, and the entire school community, we recognize that we will need many more assessment tools to accurately meet their needs. In this chapter, we will discuss the sixth and final element of the MMECCA framework, **ASSESSMENT** for instruction, which illustrates the nature of assessment and its relationship to student evaluation, describes a variety of assessment options that you can use during the teaching process and to inform instruction, and provides innovative approaches for assessing student learning. These techniques have proven to be beneficial in assessing student learning for all students, especially English language learners, students from culturally diverse backgrounds, and students with disabilities.

We begin this conversation about assessment in diverse, standards-based classrooms with the concept of equity pedagogy. Marshall (2002) defines this term as a "dimension of multicultural education," that is "based on the premise that all students can learn" (p. 25). In this concept, he also embeds the idea that when teachers implement a variety of teaching techniques and methods "to facilitate the academic achievement of all students" (p. 25), they will also use a range of assessment techniques and measures to document what and how students learn. Marshall (2002) also believes that learning about each student is fundamental for helping all educators achieve their goals. With this concept of equity pedagogy defined, we now proceed with our discussion of assessment.

Analyzing the Nature of Assessment

When multiple sources of purposeful information about students are gathered and used to inform instruction, assessment can take place (Vacca & Vacca, 2008). Given our current educational climate, high-stakes testing has become the driving force behind instruction in many school districts. The data from statewide testing tend to be "used not only as assessment information about students' progress, but also as a way to 'grade' schools, draw inferences about teachers, and provide typical one-time incentives to school districts to reform" (Duplass, 2006, p. 264).

Two major types of testing include norm-referenced and criterion-referenced tests. Norm-referenced tests compare a student's performance with other students, and criterion-referenced tests measure a student's performance based on specified criteria. Obtaining a driver's license is an example of a criterion-referenced test, and the Stanford Achievement Test (SAT) is an example of a norm-referenced test. Both tests can be standardized so that students can take them under the same conditions. Figure 6.1 outlines characteristics for norm-referenced and criterion-referenced testing.

High-stakes standardized tests are norm-referenced tests that have a particular purpose. The scoring information is returned to individual districts, and the results show teachers how their students performed in relationship to a nationally normed group. Typically, these instruments provide meager diagnostic information that rarely assists teachers in their classrooms.

FIGURE 6.1
Comparing Norm-Referenced and Criterion-Referenced Testing

	Norm-Referenced Testing	Criterion-Referenced Testing
Principal Use	Survey Testing	Mastery Testing
Major Emphasis	• Measures individual differences in student achievement	• Describes tasks that students can perform
Interpretation of Results	• Compares performance to that of other individuals	• Compares student performance to a clearly specified achievement domain
Content Coverage	• Typically covers a broad area of achievement	• Typically focuses on a limited set of learning tasks
Nature of Test Plan	• Uses a table of specifications	• Uses detailed domain specifications mostly
Item Selection Procedures	• Items are selected to specifically obtain a reliable ranking • Easy items are typically eliminated	• Includes all items needed to adequately describe performance • No specific items are altered to increase the spread of scores
Performance Standards	• The level of performance is determined by the student's *relative* position in some known group (e.g., He ranks 5th in a group of 20 students)	• The level of the student's performance is usually determined by absolute standards (e.g., She demonstrates mastery by defining 90 percent of the technical terms on this test)

Two other descriptors that are often used with testing are summative and formative assessments. An end-of-the-year achievement test is an example of a summative assessment. Although many norm-referenced tests are summative in nature, criterion-referenced tests can also be summative if they occur at the end of a teaching-learning experience (Duplass, 2006). Performance and portfolio assessments are also assessments that teachers can use in their classrooms. Performance assessments are usually curriculum-based and ask students to construct responses on real-world tasks. Portfolio assessments are also curriculum-based and consist of student products and other information collected over time (Duplass, 2006).

According to Daws and Singh (1999 in Duplass, 2006), there are two primary purposes for assessment. The first purpose is "to provide teachers and students with information and insight into students' success or failure in the learning process," and the second purpose is, "to provide teachers with feedback on their teaching effectiveness or ineffectiveness" (p. 263). Ultimately, assessment answers the question of how well students are learning. Well-designed assessments closely parallel what many educators consider to be effective instruction (Gronlund, 2003, p. 4). Effective instruction

- Includes a clearly defined set of intended learning outcomes.
- Is congruent with the outcomes to be assessed.
- Is designed to fit the relevant student characteristics and is fair to everyone.
- Provides information that is meaningful, dependable, and relevant.
- Gives students early feedback from assessment results.
- Reveals students' learning weaknesses from the assessment results.
- Provides useful results for evaluating the appropriateness of the objectives, methods, and instructional materials.

Using Assessment to Inform Instruction

Ideally, assessment should be used to inform instruction. The struggle that we frequently face as teachers is making choices concerning the age-old dilemma of adding either depth or breadth to our instruction. With increasing demands to cover content and assess what students know, many teachers often feel that they don't have the time to gather information about students' prior knowledge, experiences, and interests that would be beneficial to their instructional delivery. We believe that a symbiotic relationship exists between improving instruction and using a variety of assessment tools. The more we know about multiple types of assessment techniques, the better equipped we will be to select the most appropriate instructional strategies to use with our students. Assessment is not something that should just be done after instruction; it should inform the process before, during, and after teaching has occurred. Figure 6.2 illustrates how assessment drives the instructional cycle. Next, we discuss the role of assessment in each phase of instruction.

FIGURE 6.2
The Instructional Cycle

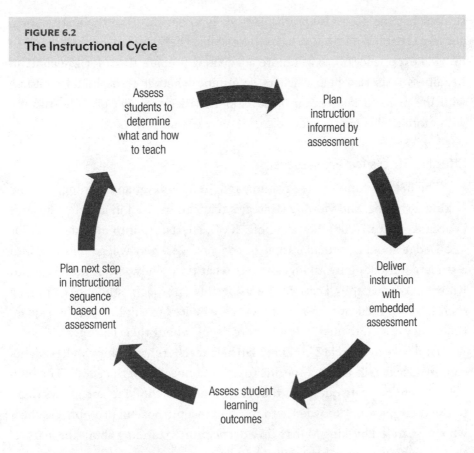

Using Assessment Before Instruction

Gronlund (2003) recommends that teachers consider the following questions before starting instruction:

1. To what extent do the students possess the skills and abilities that are needed to begin instruction?
2. To what extent have the students already achieved the intended learning outcomes of the planned instruction? (p. 5)

Teachers often ascertain students' prior mastery of content material by administering readiness tests. These assessments help teachers determine if the student has the necessary prerequisite skills to benefit from the instructional content. If students do not have these skills, then the teacher will need to provide experiences that will more adequately prepare them for the content. Readiness tests also help teachers determine whether they should continue with the planned instruction or develop activities that will provide students with more challenges (Gronlund, 2003).

Effective Tools for Pre-Assessment

The field of content-area reading and literacy has many reading, writing, talking, listening, and viewing strategies that can be used in a variety of ways (Vacca & Vacca, 2008). For example, KWL charts tap into a student's prior knowledge about a particular topic or concept. Teachers will gain insight into a students' thinking by asking students what they Know, what they Want to Know, and what they Learned. By using this approach, students can make their learning their own. When students are invited to think about these questions, they are motivated to think more deeply about their learning.

Tools like the Circle Thinking Map help teachers assess how well students can provide details about a specific topic or concept (Hyerle, 2000). The map helps teachers create questions that guide students' thinking and allows them to use their personal knowledge to respond to a purposeful prompt. Teachers who use Circle Thinking Maps gain a deeper understanding about the learner, their knowledge, and their skills. Anticipation guides are another tool that you can use with your students. These guides give students a preview of what you will teach and allow them the opportunity to make predictions about the text. This strategy sparks students' interest by providing an early context for the text and allows them to become active participants in the learning process. Teachers also can use cluster maps, fishbones, series-of-events chains, and mind maps to assess what students already know about a topic.

Student learning profiles also help teachers make decisions about what learners need in the instructional process. Gregory's 2005 study on aligning teacher and learner intelligences charts the brain processes linked to left and right hemispheres; creates tables for assessing an impressive number of learner preferences; and includes an inventory to assess your hemispheric preference, several learner profile checklists, and other charts. Many of these tables and charts can easily be adapted into learning profiles that students can complete or teachers can use as checklists. She also shows two learning preference surveys that measure the environmental, social, and personal factors that contribute to how and where learners prefer to study.

Using Assessment During Instruction

Effective teachers know that waiting until the end of an instructional unit to assess learning has little to no value for students. Monitoring students' learning allows both teachers and students to understand where they are in the process. Traditional forms of assessment include essay and short-answer exams, fill-in-the-blank and completion test items, true and false items, multiple-choice tests, and matching tests (Duplass, 2006). Alternatives to traditional testing include classroom jeopardy, pupil-produced tests, take-home tests, crossword puzzles, and word scrambles. Many teachers also use oral assessments like think-alouds, read-alouds, or a modified oral cloze, and written assessments like observations, checklists, rubrics, logs, journals, sketchbooks, question-answering routines, modified cloze paragraphs, and vocabulary four squares. These assessments help teachers ascertain what students know and still need to know. Tools like the Cornell Notetaking method can help teachers assess how students take notes during lectures or when viewing visual information, and how students identify main and central ideas, supporting details, and cause-and-effect relationships.

Using Assessment After Instruction

Traditionally, educators use assessments after instruction to determine learning outcomes for their students. Many of the assessment strategies that we have previously discussed can be used after instruction. It is important to remember that in inclusive classrooms, assessment strategies used for evaluating students' learning should be adapted to meet students' needs. Students should also play an active role in assessing their own learning.

Student self-assessments are one way to evaluate learning after instruction. Hernandez Sheets (2005) asserts that teacher assessments and student self-evaluation skills are mutually dependent and inseparable in the teaching-learning processes. As students internalize that assessing their knowledge growth leads to deeper overall understanding of the learning process, their motivation to succeed and their enthusiasm in teaching-learning events gradually increases. Students who develop and practice metacognitive skills take a more active role in the teaching-learning process (Hernandez Sheets, 2005). We want students to develop the ability and desire to discuss and critique their own understanding and acquisition of knowledge. Hernandez Sheets (2005) states that students should become adept at setting realistic and attainable goals and making candid evaluations of their performance. As students monitor their progress and performance, their self-esteem will increase and they will develop into self-regulated learners.

Grading is another important issue to be considered when assessing student learning outcomes. To some extent, grades are intended to communicate how students are performing academically. Although standards-based reforms provide clear outcomes for what is important for students to learn and what skills they need, Guskey (2008) believes that educators must view the process systemically. He recommends that educators should avoid the following pitfalls when grading:

- Grading on the curve
- Selecting only one class valedictorian
- Using grades as a form of punishment
- Using zeros in grading
- Drawing from too many different sources of evidence to determine students' grades

Practices such as these can threaten the validity of grades and undermine student morale. Although these practices may sound very straightforward, we recognize that it is difficult to remain completely unbiased when scoring a student's performance. Other factors such as the personal relationships between students and teachers or teachers and parents can unduly influence the assessment process. As teachers, we need to heighten our self-awareness to avoid skewing a student's assessments or grades.

Using Assessments with Diverse Students

Grant and Sleeter (2007) recommend the following general considerations for assessing diverse students:

- Use inferences from multiple and balanced sources of evidence versus using one single source of evidence.
- Evaluate students' performances with established criteria instead of comparing students' performance with other students.
- Balance evidence compiled from other teachers and outside sources instead of solely relying on outside sources.
- Use a wider range of context-based, complex tasks that can be used with multiple approaches and solutions instead of only using assessment items that are short, skill-focused, single-answer, and decontextualized. (pp. 207–208)

Grant and Sleeter (2007) also suggest that teachers use authentic assessments that allow students to engage in actions and processes that approximate real-world tasks. Authentic assessments reflect many of the qualities noted in the previous list and encourage teachers to be actively involved in the assessment process. These types of assessments give teachers the opportunity to look closely at individual students and measure their content growth by comparing the student's work to their own previous work rather than to the work of other students.

Performance assessments are authentic assessments that allow teachers to determine how well a student has internalized the teaching and learning process and the content. At a glance, performance assessments allow us to make a quick determination of a student's skills. For example, if we want to know whether students can locate specific information on a computer, we can provide them with questions and tell them to perform a Web search to locate sites that will answer the given question. To assess whether students can read fluently, we can ask them to read a selection and listen to them as they read. To understand how students work to solve mathematical problems, we can engage them in a think-aloud activity and listen for how they solve the problem. In all of these instances, by observing the students' performance, we gain a sense of what learners can do. Depending on the task and the level of complexity, we can gauge students' understanding and skill. When a task is carefully constructed around our intended outcomes for our students, we will know if the learners have met the desired standard.

Portfolios are another type of authentic assessment that benefits all students, and they are especially critical for documenting the learning growth for diverse students. Portfolios are a purposeful collection of student work that demonstrates the progression of a student's skills or abilities. They can be created by using a rubric and stored in a hard-copy or electronic file. As students work on their statement of purpose for their portfolio, outline the contents for their portfolio, develop criteria for selecting their work samples, and evaluate their work samples, they are automatically engaged in higher-order thinking skills such as analysis, synthesis, and evaluation. Portfolios are not designed to compare or pit students against one another. Instead, the process should honor all students and encourage them to be thoughtful learners. Portfolios allow teachers and students to focus on how they are meeting their goals and give teachers a more holistic and positive impression of their students. Aside from these general suggestions, the following discussion provides the historical context and rationale for providing modifications for students with disabilities and English language learners and includes specific modifications that you can implement in your classroom.

Rethinking and Re-evaluating How We Provide Modifications for Students with Disabilities

The statement "Fair isn't always equal" makes us think about the following question: "What implications does this assertion hold for me and my students?" Many special education teachers know firsthand how true this statement is; however, when the federal mandates for inclusion arrived, this way of thinking was foreign to most general education teachers. Prior to inclusion mandates, special education teachers carefully assessed each student with disabilities; created educational benchmarks for each student's intellectual, social, or physical behaviors; coordinated these benchmarks with the student's IEP; and ensured that all teachers and the student understood the child's needs. Meanwhile, most general education teachers had limited understanding and training about assessing students with disabilities from their teacher education or professional development programs and would be likely to give all students identical tests in the same fashion and simply record the results. Assessing all students similarly would probably produce a modified bell curve where some students would perform extremely well, some would have average performance, and others would not do well at all.

Historically, teaching and assessing students at the middle of the bell curve was the dominant practice for general education teachers. However, with the introduction of concepts like Howard Gardner's theory on multiple intelligences (1999, 2006) and Carol Tomlinson's (1999) ideas about differentiated instruction, teachers were prompted to reconsider how their beliefs and values about equity, assessment, and evaluation coincided with these new pedagogical ideas. Many early childhood and elementary teachers welcomed these new concepts and worked to gain a comprehensive understanding about how students learn and how they could motivate them to excel. Conversely, in secondary schools where hierarchical evaluations and individual recognition are often germane to the school culture, the reception for these new ideas was quite different. While some teachers may have been sympathetic to the concept of equity, they were plagued by the uncertainty of how and if the concept of "fair isn't always equal" would work in their classroom settings.

New inclusion mandates and pedagogical ideas forced many general education teachers to rethink their traditional assessment and grading practices. Some teachers felt that it was unfair to be mandated to make accommodations. No doubt many teachers wondered, "What will Billy's parents think if they knew Sam received more time taking his quizzes?" or "What will Sonya think when Victor gets to use a word box to answer questions and she doesn't?"

Rethinking and Re-evaluating How We Provide Modifications for English Language Learners

Groundbreaking legislation and the rapid rise in minority populations also compelled general education teachers to re-evaluate how they taught English language learners. In *Lau v. Nichols* (1974), the U.S. Supreme Court ruled that Chinese-speaking students in a California school district had the constitutional right to "receive instruction in a language they can understand," regardless of their English proficiency (Marshall, 2002, p. 135). This ruling was based on the landmark case of *Brown v. Board of Education* (1954). In both cases, the defendants argued that school districts were violating the Equal Protection Clause of the 14th Amendment by not providing students with equal educational opportunities.

Prior to recent professional development courses, most general education teachers did not understand that English language learners communicate differently in the classroom than they do with their peers on the playground. Many teachers believed that if their ELLs appeared to have conversational English skills that they were equipped to handle more complex content-based language in the classroom. However, many English language learners were only able to communicate casually and informally at the Basic Interpersonal Communication Skill (BICS) level of communication as opposed to the Cognitive Academic Language Proficiency (CALP) level of communication that is required for comprehending formal academic language and text (see Hakuta, Butler, & Witt, 2000, in Garcia, 2003, for a more detailed explanation of language acquisition for English language learners). In many instances, English language learners had high levels of stress because they were simultaneously trying to learn English, develop speaking and writing proficiency, and learn specific terms related to content. Hakuta and colleagues (2000) noted that it would take four to seven years for English language learners to acquire academic language while Garcia (2003) stated that students could take as long as 10 years to gain academic language depending on their mastery of their native language. The following sections provide specific modifications that you can use in your classroom with students with disabilities and English language learners.

Implementing Assessment Modifications for Students with Disabilities

The five most widely accepted accommodation categories for students with disabilities are as follows:

1. **Presentations**—Teachers can give students Braille text or text with enlarged print, use read-alouds, provide sign interpretation, and clarify directions for students as needed.

2. **Equipment and Materials**—Teachers can give students devices with added amplification or supplement the lesson with audio or video-cassettes, calculators, or magnification.

3. **Scheduling and Timing**—Teachers can give students more time, extend their testing over multiple days or during times that the student prefers, or allow students to have multiple breaks.

4. **Response**—Teachers can have students respond to their assignments by using computers, scribes, or spell checkers.

5. **Setting**—The teacher can administer an assessment for a student individually, in a small-group setting, in a separate testing room, or at a student's home. (Mastropieri & Scruggs, 2007)

You can also modify the format of criterion-referenced tests for students with disabilities by using the following suggestions:

1. **True-False Items**
   - Write out the words true and false
   - Avoid using double negatives or emphasizing negative words in bold or with underlining

2. **Multiple-Choice Tests**
   - Reduce the number of options
   - Limit the number of confusing options (e.g., A and B but NOT C)
   - Allow students to write their answers directly on the test

3. **Short Answer Questions**
   - Allow students to circle the correct answer instead of filling in a blank

4. **Essay Questions**
   - Clearly describe what you would like to see in the students' essays and provide recommendations for how the answer should be organized. (Mastropieri & Scruggs, 2007, p. 278)

You can also choose to modify the scoring procedures or give partial credit for answers that are incorrect but indicate that the student has some knowledge of the content.

Implementing Assessment Modifications
for English Language Learners

Garcia (2003) recommends using alternative forms of assessment with English language learners, such as checklists, rating scales, cloze tests, portfolios, oral and written retells, and formal writing to address and meet their language development needs. The self-assessment tool in Figure 6.3 can help you evaluate the practices that you use to help ELLs develop their formal academic language and comprehend text. Ariza (2006) and Diaz-Rico (2004) recommend the following assessment modification tips for ELLs:

- Allow students to have more time to think about and respond to questions.
- Allow students to have additional testing time beyond the timeframe recommended in the testing guidelines.
- Provide dictionaries to students in English and in their native language.
- Ask for assistance from the bilingual or ESOL teacher when students are testing. Give students a choice to receive additional assistance in another setting outside their classroom.
- Read test directions in the student's first language.
- Be proactive and locate a person either in or outside of the school who can translate task directions and make them more comprehensible to the student.
- Include a variety of visual materials, such as drawings, cartoons, diagrams, and other graphic representations to help aid the student's comprehension.

• • •

Assessment is unquestionably an integral part of the instructional cycle. Without strong assessment, we cannot determine what or how we should teach, how well our instruction is going, or how much our students have learned. In many ways, assessment lights our path as we move through the instructional journey. Without assessment, we would be lost.

FIGURE 6.3

Teacher Self-Assessment Tool for CALP Instruction for English Language Learners

PRE-READING ACTIVITIES

	Usually	Sometimes	Rarely
1. Are my activities motivating?			
2. Do I activate or build students' background knowledge?			
3. Do I provide text-specific knowledge for my students?			
4. Do I relate the reading to my students' lives?			
5. Do I pre-teach vocabulary to my students?			
6. Do I pre-teach concepts to my students?			
7. Do I encourage my students to use questions, predict outcomes, and set the purpose?			
8. Do I allow students to use their native language?			
9. Do I seek out students and their community as resources?			
10. Do I suggest strategies for students to use?			

DURING READING ACTIVITIES

	Usually	Sometimes	Rarely
1. Do I allow my students to read silently?			
2. Do I read to my students?			
3. Do I use guided reading with my students?			
4. Do I allow my students to read orally?			
5. Do I modify the text that students are reading?			

(continued on next page)

FIGURE 6.3
Teacher Self-Assessment Tool for CALP Instruction
for English Language Learners *(con't)*

POST-READING ACTIVITIES

	Usually	Sometimes	Rarely
1. Do I question aspects of the text with my students?			
2. Do I encourage my students to discuss the text?			
3. Do I build connections between the text, my students, and the world?			
4. Do I include writing in my post-reading activities?			
5. Do I include dramatic elements in my post-reading activities?			
6. Do I include artistic, graphic, and non-verbal elements in my post-reading activities?			
7. Do I encourage my students to apply what they read and do outreach activities?			
8. Do I re-teach concepts that my students do not understand?			

Adapted from Graves, M. F., & Fitzgerald, J. (2003). Scaffolding reading experiences for multilingual classrooms. In G. G. Garcia (Ed.) *English learning: Reaching the highest level of English literacy* (p. 102). Copyright 2003 by the International Reading Association. www.reading.org.

Resources for Assessment

BOOKS

Blaz, D. (2008). *Differentiated assessment for middle and high school classrooms*. Larchmont, NY: Eye on Education.

Salend, S. J. (2009). *Classroom testing and assessment for ALL students: Beyond standardization*. Thousand Oaks, CA: Corwin.

Thurlow, M. L., Elliott, J. L., & Ysseldyke, J. E. (2003). *Testing students with disabilities: Practical strategies for complying with district and state requirements*. Thousand Oaks, CA: Corwin.

Ysseldyke, J., & Algozzine, B. (2006). *Effective assessment for students with special needs. A practical guide for every teacher*. Thousand Oaks, CA: Corwin.

JOURNAL ARTICLES

Cox-Petersen, A., & Olson, J. K. (2007). Alternate assessments for English language learners: Using drawings and interviews to measure student learning. *Science and Children, 44*(6), 46–48.

Edgemon, E. A., Jablonski, B. R., & Lloyd, J. W. (2006). Large-scale assessments: A teacher's guide to making decisions about accommodations. *Teaching Exceptional Children, 38*(3), 6–11.

Rieck, W. A., & Wadsworth, D. E. (2005). Assessment accommodations: Helping students with exceptional learning needs. *Intervention in School and Clinic, 41,* 105–109.

Rogers, C., & Helman, L. (2009). One size does not fit all: How assessment guides instruction in word study with English language learners. *The New England Reading Association Journal, 44*(2), 17–22.

Salend, S. J. (2009). Technology-based classroom assessments: Alternatives to testing. *Teaching Exceptional Children, 41*(6), 48–58.

Siegel, M. A., Wissehr, C., & Halverson, K. (2008). Sounds like success: A framework for equitable assessment. *The Science Teacher, 75*(3), 43–46.

Willner, L. S., Rivera, C., & Acosta, B. D. (2009). Ensuring accommodations used in content assessments are responsive to English language learners. *The Reading Teacher, 62,* 696–698.

7

Putting It All Together

Integrating all the ideas that we discussed in this book into your own classroom may seem daunting at first. However, taking the process one step at a time will be easier than trying to implement all of the ideas at once. In this chapter, we lay out a number of important steps that you may want to consider as you move forward. As you begin this journey, consider the following three things first:

1. Know the content
2. Know your students
3. Know yourself

Know the Content

Do not overlook the significance of knowing your content. While it is certainly necessary to understand the content standards for your grade levels and content areas, this knowledge alone is not sufficient. Teaching new information to someone else, particularly struggling learners, requires that we have a deep and broad knowledge of the content. For example, if you are a math teacher, it is not enough to know how to apply a particular algorithm. You also must know why it works and be able to explain it in such a way that your students can understand. You should also be aware of conceptual gaps and common misconceptions that often derail naïve learners. As discussed in Chapter 4, teachers also must be able to identify the big ideas or themes embedded in the content. Teachers should know how to explain to students how big ideas in various subject areas are related, tell students why the content is worth knowing, and have the ability to evaluate the content from different perspectives. For example, if you are a history teacher and you are teaching a unit on the Westward Movement in the United States, you will need to share with your students how this time period evoked different emotions for frontiersmen and Native Americans. You also need to keep in mind the content for the grade levels that are above and below the level that you teach. You will also need to know the prerequisite knowledge and skills on which your grade-level content is built as well as the knowledge and skills it will later support.

In addition to having a broad and deep knowledge of the established curriculum, teachers also must be aware of important omissions in the curriculum. Multicultural education is an area that is often overlooked, even though it is critically important in an inclusive classroom. Style (1996) argues that the curriculum should serve as both a window and a mirror for students—a window into a world that is different from their own and a mirror that reflects their image. Students also learn more when they can see themselves in the curriculum. By infusing multicultural concepts in the classroom, the curriculum can be a better reflection of the diverse groups of students that populate today's schools. Teachers also need to have knowledge about multicultural concepts.

Know Your Students

You cannot effectively teach your students if you do not know them. We must take the time to learn where each student is on the continuum of the knowledge and skills for each unit we teach and seek resources outside of the traditional curriculum that students might need. In Chapter 4, we discussed that some students may need to be taught "learning how to learn" strategies or self-management strategies. To move students along the continuum of skills expeditiously, teachers also need to know how each student learns best and what instructional materials best facilitate their learning (see Chapter 2 for instructional materials and Chapter 6 for assessment strategies that support diverse students' learning).

In addition to knowing your students academically, it is also important to understand who they are as individuals outside of the classroom. Knowing about your students' strengths, interests, and life experiences can help you plan instruction that connects your students with the content. In Chapter 5, we highlight the importance of understanding your students' community, families, and parents, and we provide strategies for gathering information about parents and families.

Know Yourself

In addition to knowing your content and knowing your students, you also must know yourself. You also need to be aware of your own strengths, needs, and teaching characteristics. You can begin by asking yourself the following questions:

- Do I have an in-depth knowledge of my content?
- Do I know about the multicultural concepts that should be infused into my classroom?
- Do I know each of my students' strengths, needs, and learning characteristics?
- Do I know how to assess and use instructional materials that embrace diverse learners (e.g., assistive technology or multicultural literature)?
- Do I use instructional methods that embrace diverse learners (e.g., multiple intelligences or cooperative learning)?
- What kind of learning climate have I established in my classroom?
- Am I able to work effectively with other teachers and parents to meet the needs of diverse learners?
- What dispositions or personal traits do I have that may facilitate the inclusion of diverse learners in my classroom (e.g., flexibility, tolerance, or a willingness to do things differently)?

Let's take a look at how Ms. Harris, a 25-year teaching veteran, adapts to change at her school.

Ms. Harris is a 6th grade science teacher at Hope Middle School. Hope Middle is a culturally and linguistically diverse school serving students from middle- and low- income backgrounds. Ms. Harris is a 25-year teaching veteran who has been described as a no-nonsense teacher who seldom embraces change. She is a committed educator who is widely respected by the building administrators, students, parents, and other teachers. Ms. Harris has excellent content knowledge in the sciences, prefers a whole-group lecture format, and has amassed an impressive array of interactive, well-organized, and content-rich lectures. She holds high standards for learning and behavior in her classroom. While many students rise to these standards, far too many students do not. This has become a great concern to Ms. Harris.

With encouragement from the district, Hope Middle School is moving forward with including more diverse students into their classrooms. During the spring of last school year, the principal announced a set of training and planning sessions focused on inclusion and integrating larger numbers of students with disabilities in general education classes through a co-teaching model. Likewise, ELL students also will be integrated into general education classes with the support of the ELL teacher. Ms. Harris was not excited at all about Hope Middle School moving toward a more inclusive model of education.

Despite Ms. Harris's many strengths, like all teachers, she also has areas of need that have to change as the task of teaching evolves. As Ms. Harris embarks upon the process of becoming a more inclusive educator, she will also need to reassess her areas of strength and need. Figure 7.1 includes a set of reflection questions that educators can use to guide them through the process of evaluating their skills.

Being aware of your strengths, needs, and teaching characteristics will also help you identify the areas in which you can be resourceful to your colleagues. Likewise, having this knowledge will also allow you to identify the areas in which you need to seek out more assistance and support.

FIGURE 7.1

Reflection Questions for Teachers

Rate the items below using the following scale.

1-Strongly Disagree   2-Disagree   3-Undecided   4-Agree   5-Strongly Agree

	1	2	3	4	5
1. I have a deep and broad knowledge of the content I teach.					
2. I know additional content that may need to be infused into the curriculum (e.g., multicultural concepts or learning strategies).					
3. I know where each of my students is on the continuum of knowledge and skills that will be taught.					
4. I know how each of my students learns best.					
5. I know each of my students' interests and life experiences.					
6. I know about my students' families and communities.					
7. I use a variety of instructional methods to embrace diverse learners (e.g., graphic organizers, multiple intelligences, cooperative learning, tiered lessons, or learning centers).					
8. I use a variety of instructional materials to embrace diverse learners (e.g., assistive technology, Internet-based materials, iPods, MP3 players, bilingual materials, and multicultural literature).					
9. I have established an inclusive classroom ethos that helps all students respect every individual's differences.					
10. I use behavior management strategies that help all students respect every individual's differences.					
11. I can move all of my students along the continuum of skills and help them master established standards from my state or school district.					
12. I infuse additional content into the curriculum that embraces the needs of diverse learners (e.g., multicultural concepts and learning strategies).					
13. I effectively engage in collaborative roles with other teachers to promote the educational success of diverse learners (e.g., using co-teaching for collaborative problem solving).					
14. I work effectively with diverse parents and families to promote the educational success of diverse students.					
15. I use assessment to determine what and how to teach.					
16. I use a variety of assessment strategies to assess student learning (e.g., project-based assignments, performance activities, portfolio assessment, and student self-assessment).					
17. I use assessment accommodations and modifications as appropriate.					

Delivering Instruction to Your Students

Once you are comfortable with your knowledge of the content, your students, and yourself, you can begin focusing on delivering instruction. Rather than trying to make radical and sudden changes in this area, use a more incremental approach. The following discussion presents ideas for setting the stage for instruction, selecting instructional methods and materials, and reassessing and adjusting instructional strategies.

Setting the Stage and Planning for Instruction

Designing the physical environment of the classroom is an important first step for setting the stage for instruction. If it is the beginning of the school year and you are open to more radical changes in your classroom, consider some of the suggestions from Chapter 3, such as experimenting with the seating arrangements or allowing students to help create the classroom rules. If you are in the latter part of the school year and don't want to make major changes to your physical space, begin by adding more diverse pictures or other multicultural items into the classroom displays and bulletin boards. As noted in Chapter 3, all students should be able to see themselves reflected in the classroom. Organizing your physical environment will allow you to efficiently utilize the instructional methods you use the most and facilitate your interactions with your diverse students.

Of course, the physical arrangement is only one aspect of the classroom environment. As educators, we also need to think about the classroom climate and ethos. Chapter 3 highlights important aspects about creating an effective classroom climate such as behavior management, interaction styles, and responding to diversity. Again, it is easier to make significant changes in these elements at the beginning of the school year or after a long break.

Selecting Instructional Methods and Materials

Selecting instructional methods and materials will depend upon who the students are and what is being taught, your own instructional style, and your level of confidence with various instructional methods and materials.

It would probably be overwhelming to attempt to make dramatic changes in your teaching methods overnight. If you are a veteran teacher like Ms. Harris, you may want to begin by tweaking your whole-group lecture format versus immediately using tiered lesson plans. You can also think about developing powerful lectures that focus on big ideas (see Chapter 4), supplementing lectures with graphic organizers, integrating multiple intelligences into your lesson plans (see Chapter 1), and enhancing your curriculum with audiobooks, MP3 players, and virtual tours (see Chapter 2). If your school is moving toward integrating more inclusive models into the classroom, you may want to begin co-planning meetings with the special education teachers, co-teachers, or specialists at your school (see Chapter 5). These meetings will allow you and your colleagues to discuss how to pre-teach concepts with your students and reinforce ideas and concepts through post-teaching. As the co-teaching relationship develops, you and your colleagues may begin to share instructional responsibilities in your classroom. While teaching roles may still differ (e.g., the specialist is responsible for teaching learning strategies to the students and the general education teacher focuses on the content), there is instructional equity in the classroom, and every student views each teacher as a legitimate instructor for the entire class.

As you explore teaching methods that embrace diverse learners, you can begin to supplement your instruction with mini-lessons. If you are using a co-teaching model at your school, the special education teacher or ESL specialist can help you implement these lessons. You can also phase in cooperative learning strategies with your students. Students can work on the same tasks within each group, and you can assign various roles to students based on their learning characteristics. When you begin integrating cooperative learning groups into your classroom, start with small groups of two to three students. As your students become more confident with this approach, you can increase the group size to five to six students per group.

Next, you may want to consider experimenting with tiered lessons and learning centers based on your students' learning characteristics and needs. These two methods can be more complex than the methods discussed thus far. In tiered lessons, each lesson tier will involve a different process, product, or learning outcome to allow students to do something different at each stage.

With learning centers, teachers can use this process to specifically embrace diverse learners by differentiating their learning across and within several learning center stations.

Reassessing and Adjusting Your Teaching Methods

As with anything in life, practice makes perfect. Your first attempt at some of the strategies we shared in the book may not be met with immediate overwhelming success. If you are like most teachers, it will take time to refine your practice, become comfortable with using a new approach, and help your students feel confident using strategies that are different from those you may have used with them in the past. After this period of adjustment, however, it is important for you to assess the impact of your instruction on your students' learning. You will need to discover what is and isn't working for you and your students. Furthermore, if something isn't working, it is helpful to determine why. Using varied and differentiated assessment strategies is helpful for evaluating your students' learning needs and determining the impact of your instruction. You can gain insight into why a particular strategy is or is not working by incorporating strategies such as observation, work sample analysis, student interviews, and student questionnaires. As we return to Ms. Harris and her transition with more diverse students at Hope Middle School, you can see how she and her colleagues applied these strategies to investigate what worked, what did not work, and why. The next part of this scenario shows how she refined her teaching methods to better meet the needs of the diverse learners in her classroom $1^1/_2$ years later.

Ms. Harris was not excited at all about Hope Middle School moving toward a more inclusive model of education. Her principal stated that this move would ultimately mean that more English language learners and students with disabilities would be integrated into her classes during the upcoming school year. This move also signaled that general education teachers, special education teachers, and ESL specialists would be expected to use a co-teaching model. Co-teaching meant that she would have to share her classroom with another adult, which is something that she had not done in her entire 25-year teaching career. Additionally, all of these changes were set to occur at the same time that teachers at Hope were under the gun to meet the state's standards and be monitored by accountability assessments. Faced with these changes, Ms. Harris felt overwhelmed and apprehensive about the upcoming school year.

The only bright spot Ms. Harris saw was that the faculty would have the opportunity during the spring and summer to plan for the upcoming year. Her principal arranged for a number of professional development opportunities, which included discussing books in reading groups, visiting other schools with diverse populations of students in inclusive settings, completing self-assessments, and creating individualized professional development plans (see Figures 7.1 and 7.2 for examples of self-assessments and individual professional development plans). Based on these activities, additional professional development opportunities would be available to teachers during the summer. Finally, the principal and teacher planning teams developed plans during the summer to smoothly integrate students with disabilities into general education classes. These plans included aligning teachers' schedules to allow teaching teams to have common planning periods and building in time for special education teachers and ESL specialists to co-teach in classes as needed. Ms. Harris participated in all of these professional development and planning activities.

For her individual professional development goals, Ms. Harris decided that she wanted to learn more about integrating multicultural concepts and learning strategies into the curriculum, using more instructional methods that embrace diverse learners, and working with collaborative teaching roles. To address these goals, Ms. Harris participated in a range of activities. During the summer, she read and discussed books with her colleagues. The following school year, she visited the classrooms of teachers with expertise in her areas of need. She also participated in lesson study groups and peer coaching teams.

After that first spring and summer of planning and professional development, Hope Middle School began to move larger numbers of ELLs and students with disabilities into general education classrooms. Although Ms. Harris had learned a lot over the preceding spring and summer, she was still a bit apprehensive. She didn't think it would be a good idea to try to do everything she had been studying about all at once, so she decided

(text continued on p. 141)

FIGURE 7.2
Sample Individual Professional Development Plan

Part I

Based on your self-assessment, please identify three professional development goals for the next year.

Goal 1_____

Goal 2_____

Goal 3_____

Part II

For each goal identified above, please circle the method of professional development below that you would prefer. Circle as many methods of professional development as you would like for each goal.

Goal 1

Workshop or seminar	Reading Group	Peer Coaching	Lesson Study
Field trip to expert site or with expert teacher	Case Writing	Action Research	Other (please specify)

Goals 2

Workshop or seminar	Reading Group	Peer Coaching	Lesson Study
Field trip to expert site or with expert teacher	Case Writing	Action Research	Other (please specify)

Goal 3

Workshop or seminar	Reading Group	Peer Coaching	Lesson Study
Field trip to expert site or with expert teacher	Case Writing	Action Research	Other (please specify)

Part III

For each goal above, please describe how you will assess your learning. Please note the target dates for each assessment.

Goal 1

_____

_____

Target date(s)_____

Goal 2

_____

_____

Target date(s)_____

Goal 3

_____

_____

Target date(s)_____

to take a phased approach. Right away, she used various assessments to determine the learning characteristics of all her students. Prior to beginning her first unit, she determined what her students' existing knowledge and skills were relative to the content.

Ms. Harris also made sure that her physical environment reflected every student in her class. She displayed an array of photographs with scientists from multiple cultures across her front wall and included biographies of diverse scientists in her classroom library. She decided to keep her seating arrangement in rows because she anticipated using a teacher-directed lesson format for the first part of the year. She did, however, add a small table for group work and mini-lessons in the back of the room. Ms. Harris had to give up some storage space for the table, but she felt that it would be worth it in the long run.

After consulting with a special education teacher, Ms. Harris also augmented her behavior management system to better accommodate the needs of students with emotional and behavior disorders in her class. To help these students, she implemented strategies such as providing explicit guidance to students about her behavioral expectations, using a system of warnings, deescalating unwanted or negative behaviors, using cognitive behavior modification, and giving students frequent feedback on their behaviors.

Ms. Harris also immediately set a tone of respect in her classroom and clearly explained how she planned to address each student's individual differences. She made sure that her classes understood that all students would get what they needed; however, she emphasized that everyone would not get the same thing because everyone does not need the same thing. She used this strategy as a preemptive strike just in case students thought that she gave preferential treatment to some students or unfairly differentiated an assignment for other students. Ms. Harris was also conscious of modeling respect for every student's individual differences by praising them for all of their progress, whether it was academic, behavioral, or social.

Initially, Ms. Harris stuck with her tried-and-true, whole-group lecture format. However, she did tweak her methods to include graphic organizers and student learning profiles that she developed to integrate the multiple intelligences that were compatible to her students' strengths.

In her unit about how the Earth's surface changes over time, her lectures included a rap about the formation of volcanoes for musical-rhythmic learners, three-dimensional models for visual-spatial learners, and a flow chart depicting the process of change for logical-mathematics learners. Prior to this unit, Ms. Harris asked the special education teacher and ESL specialist to use mini-lessons to pre-teach related vocabulary to a small group of students in each class who needed assistance. These teachers also reviewed core concepts and vocabulary with mini-lessons at the end of the unit.

After that unit, Ms. Harris assessed the impact of her instruction on her students' learning. She compared the students' performance on the pre-assessment used at the beginning of the unit with the students' performance on the post-assessment at the end of the unit. She reviewed her observational notes and some of the students' work samples. She also chatted briefly with some of her students about their impressions of the unit. Ms. Harris determined that while more of her students successfully mastered the concepts, some students still did not. It appeared that these students lacked the prerequisite understandings for the unit. It was possible that these students needed more differentiation of the content.

By the middle of that year, Ms. Harris started to successfully integrate strategies into her instruction that allowed her to better differentiate the content to meet the needs of her students. During a unit about seasonal changes, she integrated multiple opportunities for students to engage in cooperative learning activities. She assigned specific roles that capitalized on each student's strengths or interests. Ms. Harris gave each group an assignment to develop a model that illustrated how the Earth's rotation and axial tilt influence temperature. She encouraged students with strong literacy skills to research information about the topic or to write a defense for the model, and she supported students who were more kinesthetic in taking the lead to build the model. Ms. Harris also integrated multicultural concepts into the unit by discussing how climate might affect the culture of people living in different regions of the world.

By March, Ms. Harris began incorporating tiered lesson into her classroom. During her lesson on the life cycle of a star, she included one tier for learners who still needed to work on the characteristics that differentiate stars from planets, a second tier to help students focus on a star's life cycle, and a third tier that helped students estimate the sun's position in its life cycle and predict how life on Earth would change over time based on the sun's life cycle.

At the close of the year, Ms. Harris was pleased with the progress her class made toward mastering the science concepts in the curriculum. Although her classes were more academically diverse than they were in previous years, the strategies that she employed promoted greater student achievement. She was more confident than ever before that her students would be well prepared for the end–of–the–year accountability assessments.

Timeless Wisdom for Your Journey

Undoubtedly, your journey will be different from Ms. Harris's journey. Like our students, each teacher is different. There are several lessons that you can take from Ms. Harris's journey:

- Set aside time for planning sessions and professional development to make your journey easier.
- Invite trusted colleagues to take this journey with you. It would be great for the whole school to be on board, but this is not necessary to be successful. You just need a few partners to help you bounce around your ideas.
- Make incremental changes rather than trying everything at once.
- Recognize that everything probably will not work perfectly the first time you try it. Analyze what went wrong and try it again.
- Realize that change is an ongoing process and it is critical for continued professional growth.
- You will never "arrive." There will always be things that you can learn to do better to embrace the needs of diverse students.

Wherever you are on your journey, the Teacher's Serenity Prayer is a great poem to keep in mind as you strive to meet the need of all learners.

Teacher's Serenity Prayer

Grant me the serenity to appreciate the unique gifts
and needs of each of my students;
the courage to challenge them to do their best; and
the wisdom to help them become all that they can be.

REFERENCES

Adams, C. M., & Pierce, R. L. (2003). Teaching by tiering. *Science and children, 41*(3), 30–34.

Archer, A., & Gleason, M. (1997). Direct instruction in content area reading. In D. Carnine, J. Silbert, & F. Kameenui (Eds.), *Direct instruction reading* (3rd ed.) (pp. 339–393). Columbus, OH: Merrill.

Ariza, E. N. W. (2006). *Not for ESOL teachers: What every teacher needs to know about the linguistically, culturally, and ethnically diverse student.* Boston: Pearson/Allyn and Bacon.

Armstrong, A. (2009). *Multiple intelligences in the classroom.* Alexandria, VA: ASCD.

Banks, J. A. (2001). *Cultural diversity and education: Foundations, curriculum, and teaching.* Boston: Allyn and Bacon.

Bohm, A. P., & Sleeter, C. E. (2001). Will multicultural education survive the standards movement? *Education Digest, 66*(5), 17–24.

Boyer, L., & Mainzer, R. (2003). Who's teaching students with disabilities? *Teaching Exceptional Children, 35*(6), 8–11.

Bursuck, W., & Damer, M. (2007). *Reading instruction for students who are at risk or have disabilities.* Boston: Allyn and Bacon.

Churchill, D. (2007). Web 2.0 and possibilities for educational application. *Educational Technology, 47*(2), 24–29.

Conderman, G., & Bresnahan, V. (2008). Teaching big ideas in diverse middle school classrooms. *Kappa Delta Pi Record, 44,* 176–180.

Council on Interracial Books for Children. (1978). *Identifying sexism and racism in children's books* [Kit]. New York: Author.

Cruickshank, D. R., Jenkins, D. B., & Metcalf, K. K. (2009). *The act of teaching.* (5th ed.). Boston: McGraw-Hill Higher Education.

Diamond, B., & Moore, M. (1995). *Multicultural literacy: Mirroring the reality of the classroom.* White Plains, NY: Longman.

Diaz-Rico, L. T. (2004). *Teaching English learners: Strategies and methods.* Boston: Pearson/Allyn and Bacon.

Dryfoos, J. G. (2008). Centers of hope. *Educational Leadership, 65*(7), 38–43.

Duerr, L. L. (2008). Interdisciplinary instruction. *Educational Horizons, 86,* 173–180.

Duplass, J. A. (2006). *Middle and high school teaching: Methods, standards, and best practices.* Boston: Houghton Mifflin.

Echevarria, J., Vogt, M. E., & Short, D. (2004). *Making content comprehensible for English language learners: The SIOP model.* Boston: Allyn and Bacon.

Ellis, E. S. (1997). Watering up the curriculum for adolescents with disabilities: Goals of the knowledge dimension. *Remedial and Special Education, 18,* 326–346.

Evertson, C., Emmer, E. T., & Worsham, M. E. (2006). *Classroom management for elementary teachers.* (7th ed.). Boston: Allyn & Bacon.

Fan, X. (2001). Parental involvement and students' academic achievement: A growth modeling analysis. *The Journal of Experimental Education, 70*(1), 27–61.

Figueras, B., Edwards L., & Langdon, D. (2008). Executive function and language in deaf children. *Journal of Deaf Studies and Deaf Education, 13,* 362–377.

Fisher, N., & Happe, F. (2005). A training study of theory of mind and executive function in children with autistic spectrum disorders. *Journal of Autism and Developmental Disorders, 35,* 757–771.

Friend, M. (2007). *Introduction to special education.* Boston: Allyn and Bacon.

Friend, M., & Cook, L. (2007). *Interactions: Collaboration skills for school professionals.* Boston: Pearson.

Gagnon, J. C., & Maccini, P. (2001). Preparing students with disabilities for algebra. *Teaching Exceptional Children, 34*(1), 8–15.

Garcia, G. G. (Ed.). (2003). *English learning: Reaching the highest level of English literacy.* Newark, DE: International Reading Association.

Gardner, H. (1999). *Reframing intelligences: Multiple intelligences for the 21st century.* New York: Basic.

Gardner, H. (2006). *Multiple intelligences: New horizons in theory and practice.* New York: Basic Books.

Gollnick, D., & Chinn, P. (2009). *Multicultural education in a pluralistic society* (8th ed.). Upper Saddle River, NJ: Pearson Education.

Grant, C. A., & Sleeter, C. E. (2007). *Doing multicultural education for achievement and equity.* New York: Routledge.

Grant, C. A., & Sleeter, C. E. (2008). *Turning on learning: Five approaches for multicultural teaching plans for race, class, gender, and disability.* Hoboken, NJ: Wiley.

Gregory, G. H. (2005). *Differentiating instruction with style: Aligning teacher and learner intelligences for maximum achievement.* Thousand Oaks, CA: Corwin Press.

Gronlund, N. E. (2003). *Assessment of student achievement.* (7th ed.). Boston: Allyn & Bacon.

Grossman, H. (1995). *Special education in a diverse society.* Boston: Allyn and Bacon.

Gunter, M. A., Estes, T. H., & Mintz, S. L. (2007). *Instruction: A models approach.* (5th ed.). Boston: Pearson/Allyn Bacon.

Guskey, T. R. (Ed.) (2008). *Practical solutions for serious problems in standards-based grading.* Thousand Oaks, CA: Corwin Press.

Hernandez Sheets, R. (2005). *Diversity pedagogy: Examining the role of culture in the teaching-learning process.* Boston: Allyn & Bacon.

Hyerle, D. (2000). *A field guide to using visual tools.* Lyme, NH: Designs for Thinking.

Jalongo, M. R., & Isenberg, J. P. (2004). *Exploring your role: A practitioner's introduction to early childhood education* (2nd ed.). Upper Saddle River, NJ: Pearson/Merrill/Prentice Hall.

Johnson, D., & Johnson, R. (1989). Cooperative learning: What special education teachers need to know. *The Pointer, 35,* 5–10.

Kapalka, G. (2009). *8 Steps to classroom management success: A guide for teachers of challenging students.* Thousand Oaks, CA: Corwin Press.

Kauchak, D. P., & Eggen, P. D. (2003). *Learning and teaching: Research-based methods.* (4th ed.). Boston: Allyn & Bacon.

Kellogg, R. D., & Kellough, N. G. (2007). *Secondary school teaching: A guide to methods and resources.* (3rd ed.) Upper Saddle Hill, NJ: Pearson/Merrill/Prentice Hall.

Kellough, R. D., & Carjuzaa, J. (2006). *Teaching in the middle and secondary schools.* (8th ed.). Upper Saddle River, NJ: Pearson/Merrill/Prentice Hall.

Kroth, R. L., & Edge, D. (2007). *Communicating with parents and families of exceptional children.* Denver, CO: Love Publishing.

Lazear, D. (2001). Teaching for, with, and about multiple intelligences. In A. L. Costa's *Developing minds: A resource book for teaching thinking* (3rd ed.). Upper Saddle River, NJ: Prentice Hall.

Lewis, R. B., & Doorlag, D. H. (2006). *Teaching special students in general education classrooms* (7th ed.). Upper Saddle River, NJ: Pearson/Prentice Hall.

Lustig, M., & Koestner, J. (2006). *Intercultural competence: Interpersonal communication across cultures* (5th ed.). Boston: Allyn & Bacon.

Malone, B. G., & Nelson, J. S. (2006). Standards-based reform: Panacea for the twenty-first century? *Educational Horizons, 84,* 121–128.

Manke, M. P. (1997). *Classroom power relations: Understanding student-teacher interaction.* Mahwah, NJ: Lawrence Erlbaum.

Marshall, P. L. (2002). *Cultural diversity in our schools.* Australia: Wadsworth/Thompson Learning.

Mastropieri, M. A., & Scruggs, T. E. (2007). *The inclusive classroom: Strategies for effective instruction.* (3rd ed.). Upper Saddle River, NJ: Pearson/Merrill/Prentice Hall.

Mercer, C. D., & Pullen, P. C. (2005). *Students with learning disabilities.* Upper Saddle River, NJ: Pearson Education.

Miller, S. P. (2009). *Validated practices for teaching students with diverse needs and abilities.* (2nd ed.). Upper Saddle River, NJ: Pearson Education.

Morrell, E. (2002). Toward a critical pedagogy of popular culture: Literacy development among urban youth. *Journal of Adolescent and Adult Literacy, 46*(1), 72–77.

National Center for Education Statistics. (1998). *Parent involvement in children's education: Efforts by public elementary schools.* Washington, DC: Author.

National Center for Education Statistics. (2006). *School and parent interaction by household and poverty status: 2002–03.* Washington, DC: Author.

National Center for Education Statistics. (2007). *The condition of education 2007.* Washington, DC: Author.

Nelson, B. (2006). On your mark, get set, wait! Are your teacher candidates prepared to embed assistive technology in teaching and learning? *College Student Journal, 40*(3), 485–494.

Okolo, C., Ferretti, R., & MacArthur, C. (2005). Teaching history in inclusive classrooms: Technology-based practices and tools. In C. L. Warger (Ed.), *Technology and media for accessing the curriculum: Instructional support for students with disabilities.* (pp. 1–9). Arlington, VA: Technology and Media Division of the Council for Exceptional Children.

Opitz, M. F. (1994). *Learning centers: Getting them started, keeping them going.* Boston: Scholastic.

Orkwis, R. (1999). *Curriculum access and universal design for learning.* Arlington, VA: ERIC Clearinghouse on Disabilities and Gifted Education.

Pisha, B., & Coyne, P. (2001). Smart from the start: The promise of universal design for learning. *Remedial and Special Education, 22*(4), 197–203.

Rakow, S. R. (2008). Standards-based vs. standards-embedded curriculum: Not just semantics!. *Gifted Child Today, 31*(1), 43–49.

Reeves, D. B. (2000). Standards are not enough: Essential transformations for school success. *NASSP Bulletin, 84*(620), 5–12.

Reeves, D. B. (2003). Take back the standards: A modest proposal for a quiet revolution. *Leadership, 32*(3), 16–20.

Rief, S. F. (1993). *How to reach and teach ADD/ADHD Children: Practical techniques, strategies, and interventions for helping children with attention problems and hyperactivity.* Hoboken, NJ: Jossey-Bass.

Rose, D., Meyer, A., & Hitchcock, C. (2006). *The universally designed classroom: Accessible curriculum and digital technologies.* Cambridge, MA: Harvard Education Press.

Sagarese, M., & Giannetti, C. C., (1999). Getting to the heart of safety. *Schools in the Middle, 9*(7), 7–10.

Schmidt, W. H., McKnight, C. C., Cogan, L. S., Jakwerth, P. M., & Houang, R. T. (1999). *Facing the consequences: Using TIMSS for a closer look at U.S. mathematics and science education.* New York: Springer.

Schumaker, J. B., Denton, P. H., & Deshler, D. D. (1985). *Learning strategies curriculum: The paraphrasing strategy.* Lawrence, KS: University of Kansas.

Schumaker, J. B., Nolan, S. M., & Deshler, D. D. (1991). *Learning strategies curriculum: The error monitoring strategy.* Lawrence, KS: University of Kansas.

Sharan, S., Kussell, P., Hertz-Lazarowitz, R., Bejarano, Y., Raviv, S., & Sharan, Y. (1984). *Cooperative learning in the classroom: Research in desegregated schools.* Hillside, NJ: Lawrence Erlbaum.

Shapiro, L. (1994). *The very angry day that Amy didn't have.* Wilkes-Barres, PA: Childswork/Childsplay.

Shoemaker, B. (1989). *Integrative education: A curriculum for the twenty-first century.* Eugene, OR: Oregon School Study Council.

Slavin, R. (1994). *Cooperative learning.* Boston: Allyn and Bacon.

Smith, S., & Smith, S. (2006). Leveling the playing field with technology solutions for individuals with Asperger's syndrome. *Closing the Gap, 25*(2), 13–16.

Style, E. (1996). Curriculum as window and mirror. The S.E.E.D. project on inclusive curriculum. Retrieved December 11, 2008, from www.wcwonline.org.

Thorson, S. A. (2003). *Listening to students: Reflections on secondary classroom management.* Boston: Allyn & Bacon.

Tomlinson, C. A. (1999). *The differentiated classroom: Responding to the needs of all learners.* ASCD: Alexandria, VA.

Tomlinson, C. A. (2001). Standards and the art of teaching: Crafting high-quality classrooms. *NASSP Bulletin, 85*(22), 38–47.

Utecht, J. (2007). Blogs aren't the enemy. *Technology and Learning, 27*(9), 32–36.

U.S. Census Bureau. (2007). Statistical abstract of the United States: 2008 (127th ed.). Washington, DC: Author.

U.S. Department of Education. (2004). *Amendments to the Individuals with Disabilities Education Act* (IDEA). Washington DC: Author.

U.S. Department of Education. (2007a). *The condition of education 2007.* Washington DC: Author.

U.S. Department of Education. (2007b). *Twenty-seventh annual report to Congress on the implementation of the individuals with disabilities education act.* Washington DC: Author.

U.S. Department of Education, Office of Educational Technology. (2004). *Toward a new golden age in American education: How the Internet, the law and today's students are revolutionizing expectations.* Retrieved May 1, 2009, from http://www.ed.gov/about/offices/list/os/technology/plan/2004/plan.pdf.

Vacca, R. T., & Vacca, J. L. (2008). *Content area reading: Literacy and learning across the curriculum.* (9th ed.). Boston: Pearson/Allyn & Bacon.

Vaughn, S., & Bos, C. S. (2009). *Strategies for teaching students with learning and behavior problems.* (7th ed.). Upper Saddle River, NJ: Pearson.

Voltz, D. L. (1994). Developing collaborative parent-teacher relationships with culturally diverse parents. *Intervention in School and Clinic 29*, 288–291.

Voltz, D. L. (2003). Personalized contextual instruction. *Preventing School Failure, 47*, 138–143.

Voltz, D. L. (2006). Inclusion in an era of accountability: A framework for differentiating instruction in urban standards-based classrooms. *Journal of Urban Learning, Teaching, and Research, 2*, 95–105.

Voltz, D. L., Collins, L., Patterson, J., & Sims, M. J. (2008). Preparing urban educators for the twenty-first century: What the research suggests. In Craig, C. J., & L. F. Deretchin (Eds.), *Teacher education yearbook XVI: Imagining a renaissance in teacher education.* (pp. 25–40). Lanham, MD: Rowman and Littlefield Education.

Waldron, N. L., & McLeskey, J. (1998). The effects of an inclusive school program on students with mild and severe learning disabilities. *Exceptional Children, 64*, 395–405.

Weinstein, C., Curran, M., & Tomlinson-Clarke, S. (2003). Culturally responsive classroom management: Awareness into action. *Theory into practice, 42*(4), 269–276.

Zwiers, J. (2004). *Developing academic thinking skills in grades 6–12: A handbook of multiple intelligence activities.* Menlo Park, CA: International Reading Association.

INDEX

Page numbers followed by *f* denote figures.

ABOUT THE AUTHORS

Deborah L. Voltz

Deborah L. Voltz is the director of the Center for Urban Education and associate professor in the department of Leadership, Special Education, and Foundations at the University of Alabama at Birmingham. She began her career as a special education teacher in the Birmingham, Alabama, City Schools, where she worked in inclusive educational programs. Voltz also taught at the university level in teacher preparation programs at several universities including Alabama State University, the University of Wisconsin-Milwaukee, the University of Louisville, and the University of Alabama at Birmingham. She has taught internationally at the University of Melbourne, Australia, and at the College of New Jersey's Johannesburg program in South Africa. Throughout the 25 years of her professional career, Voltz has had a passion for the education of diverse learners in inclusive settings. Through professional development programs such as Project SMILE—the Standards Movement and the Inclusion of Learners with Exceptionalities and Project CRISP—Culturally Responsive Instruction for Special Populations, Voltz has trained hundreds of pre-service and in-service teachers for instruction in diverse, inclusive environments. She also has published dozens of articles and book chapters devoted to this topic. You can contact her by phone at (205) 934-8320 or by e-mail at voltz@uab.edu.

Michele Jean Sims

Michele Jean Sims is an associate professor in the Department of Curriculum and Instruction and is an affiliate of the Center for Urban Education at the University of Alabama at Birmingham. For 20 years, she taught in a variety of public school positions and at varied education levels. She began her career as an elementary teacher and Title I/Chapter I reading teacher in the New York City board of education. In Philadelphia, she was a reading specialist at a group home for adjudicated adolescent boys and a Title I/Chapter I reading teacher at the middle and junior high school level in the Philadelphia School District. Three pivotal professional experiences continue to influence her practice—being a member of the STAR team, which is an interdisciplinary team for middle school students at-risk, her involvement as a teacher consultant in the Philadelphia Writing Project, and her graduate program at the Penn Graduate School of Education.

Throughout Sims's more than 30-year professional career, her interests remain centered around struggling learners, teacher beliefs, and the learning environments of learners and teachers. Her research and publications are focused on examining collegial settings that support collaboration in teaching and learning within and across diverse school and community contexts. Currently, she teaches courses that cover topics of adolescent literacy, secondary methods, and middle-level education. She is actively involved in UAB's Center for Urban Education's Urban Teacher Enhancement Program (UTEP). You can contact her by e-mail at mjsims@uab.edu.

Betty Nelson

Betty Nelson is an associate professor of special education and interim chair of the Department of Leadership, Special Education, and Foundations in the School of Education at the University of Alabama at Birmingham. She has taught in residential and public school programs and has been a program supervisor in public schools and at a private research institution. She has taught children within all areas of exceptionality and has taught higher education coursework which spans the entire breadth of the field.

Nelson's main focus in her teaching, research, and service is assistive and instructional technology. She believes that technology better prepares teachers to be a solid resource for their students and helps students access the general curriculum and develop skills for communication, socialization, and leisure activities. In her higher education classes she seeks to integrate dynamic and stimulating learning activities and create scenarios and opportunities that emphasize the importance of becoming lifelong learners.

Nelson gives numerous presentations and guest lectures at the local, state, national, and international levels each year. She has served as president of Technology and Media Division of the Council for Exceptional Children (TAM) and as president of the Special Education Technology Special Interest Group (SETSIG) of the International Society of Technology in Education (ISTE). You can contact her by e-mail at benelson@uab.edu.

Related ASCD Resources: Connecting Teachers, Students, and Standards

At the time of publication, the following ASCD resources were available; for the most up-to-date information about ASCD resources, go to www.ascd.org. ASCD stock numbers are noted in parentheses.

Print Products

Content-Area Conversations: How to Plan Discussion-Based Lessons for Diverse Language Learners by Douglas Fisher, Nancy Frey and Carol Rothenberg (#108035)

Educating Everybody's Children: Diverse Teaching Strategies for Diverse Learners by Robert W. Cole (#195024)

Getting Started with English Language Learners: How Educators Can Meet the Challenge by Judie Haynes (#106048)

Managing Diverse Classrooms: How to Build on Students' Cultural Strengths by Carrie Rothstein-Fisch and Elise Trumbull (#107014)

Meeting the Needs of Second Language Learners: An Educator's Guide by Judith Lessow-Hurley (#102043)

Videos and DVDs

Educating Everybody's Children (six 20- to 30-minute videotapes and two facilitator's guides) (#400228)

How to Coteach to Meet Diverse Student Needs (one 15-minute videotape) (#406057)

How to Involve All Parents in Your Diverse Community (one 15-minute DVD) (#607056)

THE WHOLE CHILD The Whole Child Initiative helps schools and communities create learning environments that allow students to be healthy, safe, engaged, supported, and challenged. To learn more about other books and resources that relate to the whole child, visit www.wholechildeducation.org.

For additional resources, visit us on the World Wide Web (http://www.ascd.org), send an e-mail message to member@ascd.org, call the ASCD Service Center (1-800-933-ASCD or 703-578-9600, then press 2), send a fax to 703-575-5400, or write to Information Services, ASCD, 1703 N. Beauregard St., Alexandria, VA 22311-1714 USA.